GUNNY

GUNNY

A Year in the Life of Bryan Gunn

David Chisnell

PARROT PUBLISHING
WYMONDHAM
NORFOLK

Dedicated to
the memory of
FRANCESCA GUNN

Acknowledgments

It's only when you come to write the 'acknowledgments' page that you begin to realise how many people are needed to put a book like this together. Writing a book may seem, at times, a very lonely and singular occupation, but without the help of a small army of people, most would never get off the ground.

My own thanks go, primarily, to Bryan, without who's support this book could never have happened. Despite his busy schedule, Bryan always made time to read or comment upon the book as it took shape. His agreement to allow me to use many photographs that were, originally, intended for private viewing only, has helped to make the book far more personal.

For the photographs themselves, I am grateful to Roger Harris, who has perfected the art of being in the right place at the right time, and I am indebted to him for allowing me to plunder his vast collection.

I am also grateful to Patricia Harvey, who managed to ignore my pages of scribbled ideas for illustrations, and always return with something far more suitable and inspired. Patricia's drawings have been a constant source of amusement during my meetings with Bryan.

I'm grateful, too, to both Ian Botham and Jeremy Goss who kindly took the time to write the introduction and preface for this book. I believe they have both managed to sum up what many people feel and think about Bryan.

Other thanks go to the BBC's 'A Question Of Sport' and Graham Boulter of Wymondham Photographic, who both kindly allowed me to use their photographs free of charge, Norwich City F.C. and The Football League for their permission and help in reproducing City's statistics and Dr. Ian Gibson from the UEA for giving up his time to talk to me.

Finally I'm grateful to Geo. R. Reeve Ltd., the printers, for their help in packaging this book and last, but not least, to my wife, Lynne, for the endless supply of hot coffee as the typewriter moved into extra time in the early hours of the morning.

Contents

	Foreword	12
	Preface	14
	Introduction	17
1	Golden Goals	25
2	Circuit Training	33
3	How Much Am I Bid?	37
4	A Piece of Fun or The Kiss of Death?	44
5	A Double Strike	49
6	An Evening With Who?	51
7	The Shutout	58
8	£100,000 Off to a Tee	60
9	And in the Green and Yellow Corner	66
10	Bayern Munich – Parts One and Two (and introducing the Green Flash)	69
11	The Question	74
12	A Date to Remember	75
13	A Little Bit of French	78
14	Finders Keepers	82
15	It's That Man Again	86
16	Inter The Unknown	92

17	Leeds At The Double	99
18	Elvis Lives – You Bet	104
19	It's The Ponytail Kid	107
20	A Big Day for Little Matthew	111
21	The Flying Scotsman	114
22	Guest Appearances	119
23	Fantasy Football	123
24	Nice Goal, Shame About The Scorer	126
25	What Me Ref?	131
26	End Results – An Interview with Dr. Ian Gibson	134
27	Final Thoughts – An Interview with Bryan Gunn	136
28	Gunn Shots	152
29	Norwich City Results 1993/1994	155

Illustrations

All photographs, including both the front and back cover, are by Roger Harris except those listed below.

All original drawings are by Patricia Harvey, who retains the copyright of same.

The photograph of Bryan Gunn on page 66 has been provided free of charge by Graham Boulter of Wymondham Photographic, Norfolk.

The photograph of Bryan Gunn on page 87 has been provided free of charge by
'A Question Of Sport', B.B.C., Manchester.

The photograph of Bryan Gunn and Jeremy Goss on page 13 is from the author's private collection.

None of the photographs or drawings may be reproduced without permission.

Foreword

It came as no great surprise to me when I first heard about this book. Dave walked from Land's End to Margate with me a couple of years ago and constantly bent my ear with stories of Bryan and the Canaries. Since then we've kept in regular contact and Dave has always kept me up to date with Bryan's latest achievements.

It was obvious to me, from the stories I was hearing, that there was a book begging to be written and who better than Dave to write it.

I would have loved to have taken part in some of Bryan's charity events, most notably the golf day and the performance of 'An Evening With Gary Lineker', but unfortunately other commitments kept me away from both. I was happy to hear, however, that some of the things I sent for auction or raffle prizes had helped to swell the fund.

My own walks for Leukaemia Research get a lot of publicity and people constantly ask me how we manage to keep walking for up to 30 miles a day for over three weeks. I never have what I feel is the complete answer for them, but I believe we came close to it on the last walk.

A few days before Bryan was due to join us for a day, his daughter Francesca died. I don't need to describe the pain and sorrow we all felt that day, but perhaps it was also that day which reminded us all why we were walking and how we managed to keep going.

If you're looking for heroes you won't find them on the walk, you find them in people like Bryan Gunn who, just six months after losing his daughter, set up a fund to help ensure that other children would live. The amount of money raised already is staggering and is a tribute to the strength of Bryan and his wife Susan. It also reflects the warmth that the people of Norfolk have in their hearts for them both.

Bryan has always been a giant on the football field, but now he has proven himself to be a giant off of it too, and I am grateful to have this opportunity to applaud him for it.

I hear he's hoping to join us for a day on this year's walk through Wales and I look forward to sharing his company once again. One word of warning though, Bryan, we take no prisoners on the walk. Ask Dave to tell you about Gary Lineker who joined us for a day, last time, and ended up being fined for limping!

Well done Bryan, good luck for the new season and the fundraising.

See you soon,

Ian Botham

Ian and Bryan team up at Jeremy Goss's Testimonial Golf Day.

Preface

When Dave first approached me to write the preface for 'Gunny', I was delighted. I know that every player at the club would have been more than happy to write such a tribute to Bryan.

Over the last two years or so, Bryan has proven himself to be the giant that we, at the club, all knew him to be. Both on and off the pitch he has been a tower of strength to us all.

His fundraising activities are legendary at Carrow Road. At home games Bryan will always arrive early to personally accept the cheques that have been brought down for his appeal. Everybody gets treated the same, from the company executive bringing down a cheque for a few thousand pounds, to the young fans handing over their pocket money. All get the same broad smile, the same warm handshake and the same genuine thanks.

Since the tragic loss of Francesca, we've all watched Bryan deal with his grief in the most dignified manner. He knows we've all been there for him and, in the same way, we know he's always there for us.

When I launched my own testimonial year this season, the one person that I knew immediately I could call upon was Bryan. Despite his own personal commitments and all the fundraising activities he's been involved with, he's always been available to help. He even gave up the chance of a day's golf at Wentworth to play in my own testimonial event.

On the pitch Bryan has, again, been outstanding this season. Some of his saves have been out of this world, and we all know how important his performances were to us during our European adventures.

Bryan remains one of the game's true gentlemen. He deserves every tribute that he receives and I'm happy to have had the chance to pay him this one.

JEREMY GOSS

Jeremy's goal against Bayern Munich helps swell
Bryan's appeal.

Gunny and the author after another 'marathon' fund raising session. Can you spot which one was running and which one was watching?

Introduction

Growing up as a lad in the sixties almost inevitably meant that your two main interests in life would be music and football. Invariably you would either be a fan of the Rolling Stones or The Beatles, whilst you also harboured a burning ambition to be the new Jimmy Greaves or Gordon Banks.

Like many of my friends I found my feet firmly planted in the category marked The Beatles and Gordon Banks. I can still remember spending long days in front of the bedroom mirror, tennis racket across my chest for a guitar, mimicking that famous John Lennon stance. Other days would find me in the back garden throwing a football onto our bungalow roof to practice catching it 'Banksie' style.

Sadly, when I stopped growing a good foot short of the crossbar and developed a singing voice that would have made Bob Dylan sound at home in the church choir, I realised my ambitions would have to change. If I couldn't be a player, then a spectator it would have to be.

As the years went by John Lennon slowly made way for Jimi Hendrix, Eric Clapton and Bruce Springsteen while Banksie was replaced by Peter Shilton, Ray Clemmence and Chris Woods. It would be untrue to claim that Norwich ever became a hotbed of musical talent to rival that of Liverpool or Motown, but as far as goalkeepers went it more than held its own. Names like Sandy Kennon, Kevin Keelan and Chris Woods ensured that a healthy respect would be paid to Carrow Road by visiting strikers.

As I followed the Canaries through their various fortunes of the 60s, 70s and 80s I always kept one eye on the goalkeeping spot and, with the exception of Kevin Keelan, managed, in one way or another, to cross paths with all the other City keepers.

In 1981 I sold my betting shop to Sandy Kennon whilst, four years later, I was selling ice-cream to Chris Woods when he lived in Poringland. Ironically, I had bought the betting shop from another ex-City footballer, Roy Hollis, who had scored regularly for the Canaries in the 1940s. Until I sold the shop to Sandy, the two had never met but, following introductions, Sandy immediately installed Roy as shop manager, thus allowing me to create my first and only City team.

Chris Woods, on the other hand, created his own team. Young faces would peer out from behind bedroom curtains as I pulled my van up, Mister Softee chimes ringing, outside Chris' house. The very sight of Chris would have youngsters appearing from behind every bush and gate in the close as he collected his 99s.

I remember turning my van into his close one Sunday morning to find Chris waiting by the side of the road surrounded by hordes of young admirers clutching souvenir programmes from the England tour of South America. As I pulled up beside him, Chris dug deep into his pockets and whispered: "Twenty-eight small ones please". Such was the price of fame!

When rumours of Chris' departure from Carrow Road began circulating there was obvious concern amongst supporters. Norwich had a long tradition of good goalkeepers and Chris was rated as one of the best. However, within a few weeks of installing Bryan as first team keeper, all such fears were soon forgotten. It was ironic that, in what appeared to be a geography lesson going wrong, Chris had to travel to Scotland to become England's number one, whilst the man who would become Scotland's first choice keeper had to make the trip in the opposite direction. Whatever else had happened one thing was certain, Mister Softee's turnover in the Poringland area had suffered a devastating blow.

My first meeting with Bryan was under very different circumstances. I was organising the sponsorship, on behalf of Coral Bookmakers, for Ian Botham's 1992 South Coast walk for Leukaemia Research which would go from Land's End to Margate. A few weeks into the campaign my wife and I

Ring out the old, ring in the new. It's all change as Mister
Softee's turnover takes a dive.

discovered that our three year old daughter, Alice, had cancer,
and, at about the same time, Bryan revealed that his daughter,
Francesca, had been diagnosed as having leukaemia.

A few weeks later Ian suggested to me that we should invite
Bryan to join the walk for a day, and this I agreed to do. At the
same time I was organising a local shop opening for Coral in
Wymondham, and I invited Bryan to come along and place a
charity bet on behalf of the ward at Addenbrookes Hospital
where both our daughters were being treated.

At our first meeting I found Bryan to be the perfect
gentleman for whom nothing was too much trouble. He
brought a signed football to the shop opening and also agreed
to attend and conduct the raffle at a race night I was organising
for Leukaemia Research. On the night itself, Bryan brought
along some personal belongings for our celebrity auction.

When I told Bryan of Ian's invitation to join the walk for a
day he was delighted and plans were made for him to join us for
a Sunday in Brighton. Tragically, a few days before we got to
Brighton, Francesca died. The entire walk was devastated by the

news, and although we carried on walking, the fun element of the walk never really returned.

A few days earlier Gary Lineker had joined us to walk for a day and he had told us of the progress his young son, George, was making in his battle against leukaemia. This good news obviously cheered everyone and we had all enjoyed the walk that day.

Following the loss of Francesca, I walked with Ian as he was being interviewed by the local radio station. The interviewer asked him how much it helped to receive good news, like that of baby George, when you were walking. For me, Ian's answer put everything into context. "It was great," he said to hear about George because, "it looks as though we've saved one". However, it was stories like that of Francesca that really spurred him on because there, "we've lost one. And who knows, if we'd started walking ten years earlier perhaps we could have saved her too". Simple words that brought tears to the eyes of all within hearing distance.

A few weeks after the walk had ended I bumped into Bryan in Sainsburys. He'd been sent out by Susan and was looking for the chicken department. We talked of how well City were doing in the league and how it looked as though this could really be their year. Bryan went on to tell me that as Norwich had no match that week he was taking Susan away for a romantic weekend in Paris. By sheer coincidence it also just happened to be the weekend when Scotland were playing France at rugby in the very same city.

Shortly before the start of last year's football season, Bryan and I teamed up to produce his weekly column for the Eastern Evening News, 'Bryan's Bet'. The idea of this book came as a natural progression from the column and I have felt privileged to be involved with it.

The intention of this book, apart from boosting Bryan's leukaemia fund even further, is to unashamedly pay tribute to Bryan for the major successes he has had both on and off the football field. It is a chance to remind ourselves of all the hard work that has gone into his fundraising and to record, for ever, some of the many achievements he has had.

Of the various sporting personalities I have met, Bryan stands in a class of his own. From our first meeting he has remained the perfect gentleman for whom nothing is too much trouble. Making round trips in excess of 100 miles to collect cheques from people who have raised funds for his appeal has become a way of life and he is, truly, the people's champion.

I am proud to have this chance to pay tribute to Bryan, via this book, and I am certain that anyone who reads it will come away with the same respect for 'Gunny' that I have.

Hope you enjoy the book.

The best way to start a new season – as last season's Player of The Year

From Golden Goals To Breaking Goals

When Bryan first announced his appeal, in April 1993, he could have had little idea of what he was unleashing onto the public. Launched under the title 'Gunn's Golden Goals', the idea was a simple one. Readers of the Eastern Evening News were asked to sponsor the Canaries for each goal that they scored between the appeal launch and the end of the season. A target of £10,000 was set and it was hoped that the sponsorship would inspire City to further success in their quest for Europe.

Since the death of Francesca, Bryan had been quietly raising money for various leukaemia charities with a minimum of publicity. Now, however, he was prepared to bang the drum in public in an attempt to create social awareness of the illness.

The initial aims of the appeal were to create funds to help assist local hospitals, and their staff, who cared for leukaemia victims. At its launch Bryan said, "It's a way of paying back the help which the doctors and nurses gave us through our difficult time".

Apart from sponsoring goals, Evening News readers were also invited to send in one-off donations. The previous Saturday had seen the country's most popular horse race, the Grand National, declared void, and readers were urged to hand over their refunded stakes.

It didn't take long for the ball to start rolling. Within days of the launch, over 50 cheques had been received and pledges totalling £62 per goal had been registered. Jumble sales had been announced and Easter egg raffles were being organised. It soon became apparent that the people of Norfolk wouldn't be content with simply sponsoring goals. In a matter of days a whole army of budding entrepreneurs were setting up events which would raise money for Bryan's appeal.

The first game City played after the appeal's launch was away to Tottenham. Unfortunately the Canaries were beaten 5-1, a result that effectively ruled out any lingering hopes of winning the championship. Although the one goal scored guaranteed some funds to the appeal, Keith Colman, who was co-ordinating the fundraising, decided that an extra incentive was needed to bring in more goals.

Accordingly, he announced that he would present a bottle of champagne to every City goal scorer between now and the end of the season. The incentive obviously did the trick. The following Wednesday saw the Canaries thump four goals past Leeds United at Carrow Road. Chris Sutton, who had just switched from defence to attack, grabbed his first league hat trick, whilst Dave Phillips slotted home the fourth. Both players immediately autographed and donated their champagne back to the appeal to be auctioned, with Dave Phillips going even further by announcing that he would undertake a bungee jump to raise yet more funds.

The appeal was now truly up and running. Within a fortnight of its launch, over £2,000 had been received by the organisers with much more pledged. The next week welcomed more donations including one from a local pools winner who sent in his entire winnings. The bidding for Chris Sutton's champagne topped £50 and freelance journalist, Martyn Graham, had shaved his head to raise another £300.

The same week saw Bryan at Addenbrookes Hospital in Cambridge, where Francesca had been treated. Together with his younger daughter, Melissa, Bryan opened a new play area for the children on Ward C2 where Francesca had stayed. Prior to launching his own appeal, much of the money Bryan had raised had been sent to Addenbrookes and, whilst he must have felt great sadness at his return to Cambridge, it may well have been at this point that Bryan realised how much good his appeal could do.

Whether that was the case or not, the following Monday it was announced that the appeal would now stay open throughout the summer. The target was reset at £20,000 and it was revealed that some major events were being lined up for the autumn.

By the first week in May the appeal had topped £7,000 and, a week later, a cheque from Solarbowl of Norwich for £1,325, took it through its original target of £10,000. The new target of £20,000 was already beginning to look somewhat unambitious.

Donations continued to flood in, fast and furious, as more and more events took place throughout the region. Pool marathons, football matches and darts competitions became commonplace as pubs and clubs competed against each other in their fundraising. Major financial institutions became involved as Barclays Bank sent in a cheque for £200 and challenged any other bank or building society to top it. Within a couple of weeks, Abbey National had done just that when, at the end of a week's activities, they handed over a cheque for £1,000.

Fundraising continued in all shapes and sizes, as did the fundraisers themselves. A group of 140 Beavers and Brownies raised over £170 by filling empty Smartie tubes with 5p pieces earned for completing jobs around the home. Even a cat and dog show was announced, with all proceeds going to the appeal.

By the end of June the appeal had reached over £22,000 and yet another new target had been set. This time the target was £60,000 and, with over £10,000 expected from the recently announced forthcoming football memorabilia auction, even this figure looked likely to be exceeded.

The first week in July saw Bryan accepting a cheque for over £500 from nine year old Samantha Johnson. Samantha had been diagnosed as having leukaemia the previous year and was now in remission. Together with her friends, Samantha had organised a fair at her school, Lingwood Junior. The cheque which she gave to Bryan took his appeal through the £25,000 barrier.

A few nights later the football auction took it to almost £40,000 and within a week another £5,000 had been added. With the gala performance of 'An Evening With Gary Lineker' still to come, together with the celebrity golf day at Sprowston, the latest target of £60,000 was again going to prove to be woefully low.

Somewhat reluctant to set new targets, the organisers admitted that they had been totally overwhelmed by the

response to the appeal. An unofficial target of £100,000 was bounced around but, by the end of the golf day, even this had been passed. A few days after the golf event the appeal became truly international when organisers received a cheque from TV journalist Martin Bell, who wrote that he had heard of the appeal whilst working in Bosnia.

The appeal had been officially due to close at the end of October, but November and December saw donations continue to pour in and Bryan remained actively involved. Accordingly, in December, the appeal was officially re-opened with no new target set. Setting targets was now impossible. Already events were being organised as far as six months away and the appeal had taken on a life of its own.

In April 1994, a year after its launch, the appeal stood at over £160,000. A far cry from the target of £10,000 set twelve months earlier. How much further it will grow is pure speculation. That it will continue to grow is in no doubt. That it will break every target it is set is also a certainty, the reason why targets are no longer set. Bookmakers throughout the city have already laid bets on it topping £250,000 by the end of 1994, and there appears to be every likelihood of them having to pay out.

From what was such a personal tragedy for Bryan and Susan, has grown a magnificent monument to their strength and devotion. Bryan will be remembered as one of City's greatest goalkeepers long after he hangs up his boots. But the Gunn family will be remembered for much longer, and for something much greater.

Circuit Training

Having decided to extend his appeal beyond that of simply asking readers of the Evening News to sponsor City goals, Bryan began to look for new ways of raising money. One of the first events he set up also turned out to be one of the most spectacular of his campaign.

Teaming up with racing car driver, Will Hoy, Bryan approached Anglia Television who agreed to arrange a television phone-in. Anglia would broadcast two questions on air, one on Bryan and the other on Will, and invite their viewers to ring in to a special number with their answers.

The names of all the callers who rang with the correct answers would be placed in a drum and the lucky winners drawn out. Prizes would include tickets to a forthcoming City home match and a ride around Snetterton circuit with Will. The appeal, itself, would benefit from the cost of the calls and everybody would end up a winner.

The idea of Bryan and Will teaming up, however, wasn't new. A few months earlier, Will had invited Bryan to join him at Snetterton on behalf on the British Heart Foundation. The idea was for Bryan to join Will as a passenger in his car for a circuit but, unfortunately, weather conditions that day were against them. Although Bryan's wife, Susan, enjoyed a circuit with Will, by the time it came to Bryan's turn the fog had settled far too low for the circuit to be completed in safety.

When Anglia said they needed a gimmick to launch the phone-in, therefore, Bryan quickly jumped at the second chance to join Will at Snetterton. When the day arrived, weather conditions were perfect and Bryan confidently slipped into the passenger seat alongside Will.

Racing cars are, of course, powerful machines and the drivers take them round the circuits at exceptionally high speeds. However, when carrying passengers, an unwritten rules states that, generally, the driver will travel at only half his normal speed.

For whatever reason, Will decided to turn a blind eye to this unwritten rule and tore out of the pits like the proverbial bat out of hell. While Bryan hung on for dear life, Will manoeuvred the car around the track as if he was competing in a Grand Prix final. Hairpins, loops and chicanes were all completed at a breathtaking speed and, when the car finally came to a shuddering halt, it was discovered that Will had completed the circuit in just two seconds outside of his lap record.

As Bryan climbed out of the car he still sported a wide grin and managed to describe the ride as "brilliant". Whether the grin hid the threat of revenge was something only Bryan would know and Will would worry about.

Anglia Television now had the perfect footage with which to launch the phone-in. Unfortunately they decided to launch it a day before the telephone number they gave out had been switched over to the quiz line. Viewers ringing in with their answers were, instead, greeted with a trailer for a forthcoming production of Aladdin, a mistake that was, perhaps, prophetic.

At the time of the car ride, Bryan may well have wished he was flying around the circuit on a magic carpet instead of in the cockpit next to Will. However, there was no magic lamp or genie to help him that day and he would, instead, have to simply grit his teeth and wait for the pantomime to end.

"Don't forget lads, half speed only."

Above: Susan helps Bryan prepare for his lap round Snetterton.

Below: Still smiling after just failing to beat the lap record.

How Much Am I Bid?

They say that giant oak trees grow from little acorns, and that was certainly the case when City supporter, Norman Pointer, came up with a novel idea for raising funds for Bryan's appeal.

Norman had been given a football by Manchester United captain, Steve Bruce, signed by all the current United squad and, rather than keep it for himself, he decided instead to offer it for auction. Norman approached Wally Webb of Radio Norfolk who was only too pleased to help. Accordingly, a couple of weeks later, Wally auctioned the ball off on his radio programme.

The phone lines were jammed as the bids came in until a final bid of £200 secured the ball. Suddenly a new and lucrative way of raising funds had become apparent, and a new idea was born.

Keith Colman, who was co-ordinating the appeal, went straight into action and wrote to every football club in the league. Each club was informed of Bryan's fund and asked to donate something towards a forthcoming football memorabilia auction.

It didn't take long for the clubs to respond and the replies were soon flooding in. Within a fortnight signed shirts and balls had been received from all around the country. Arsenal, Aston Villa and Celtic were amongst the clubs who sent in footballs, whilst shirts were received from Ian Rush, Kevin Keegan and Alan Hansen amongst others.

Amidst much fanfare, the auction was announced as taking place on Saturday, July 10th at the Norwich Sports Village. Potential bidders were encouraged to turn up with their cash and cheque books, and the excitement began to grow.

Above: The gloves come off as the auction starts.
Below: Another well worn jersey goes under the hammer.

Above: What a lot of lots!!!

Below: Dave Phillips, Lee Power, Chris Sutton and Mark Bowen join Bryan to ensure all four home countries are represented.

Top: Just some of the many items up for grabs.

Below: Two successful bidders receive their lots from Bryan.

During the eight weeks that followed, items continued to pour in on a daily basis. Obviously Bryan donated several items whilst his team mates at Carrow Road also did their bit to help. International shirts were signed and donated by Chris Sutton, Dave Phillips, Mark Bowen and Lee Power ensuring that all the home countries were represented.

The day of the auction saw the arrival of yet more goodies. Cricketing legend, Ian Botham, sent a bat from his last leukaemia walk which had been signed by all the celebrities who had joined him between Land's End and Margate. He also included a couple of signed sweatshirts from the walk which Mike Gatting, who had been around when they were collected, had added his signature to.

Unfortunately, the date of the auction clashed with that of the Lord Mayor's procession through Norwich. Always well supported, this year's procession had an added attraction - the Europe bound Canaries aboard an open-top bus. At the end of the procession the Canaries were greeted by the Lord Mayor and treated to a civic reception at the City Hall. Whilst such an occasion was a great tribute to them, this was certainly one time when Bryan really did wish he could be in two places at once.

As it turned out, Bryan managed to get to the Sports Village in time for the second half of the auction and was immediately called upon to model various items of clothing that he had donated. The bids, which had been coming in fast and furious in the first session, now seemed to intensify with Bryan's arrival. Shirt followed shirt and ball followed ball as bidders battled against each other to leave the Village with a souvenir.

As the auction drew to a close, Bryan found himself reunited with an old friend. The Canaries last match of the season had been away to Middlesborough where they had clinched third place in the league, a success that saw them qualify for Europe. To celebrate, Bryan had thrown one of his boots into the crowd. The boot had been caught by City fan Philip Blukert and had been donated back to the auction. Also on the table were the socks, shorts and jersey that Bryan had worn in the same game, although thankfully he had managed to keep those on until he reached the dressing room!

By the end of the evening the auction had raised over £10,000, lifting the appeal to over £40,000. If proof had ever been needed of how a simple idea could snowball into something far larger, then this was it. From the initial act of auctioning off a United football for £200 had come an evening of massive fundraising. As football supporters of all ages left the Village clutching their trophies, they were entitled to feel proud of themselves. Also entitled to give themselves a swift pat on the back were the many clubs who had generously donated items to the appeal.

Whilst there had always been sporting auctions up and down the country, the auction that evening stood in a class of its own. Practically every club in the league had responded positively to Bryan's appeal and donated an item for auction.

From outside the football world, donations had been received from celebrities as far apart as David Mellor and Edd the Duck. Local shops and businesses had provided lots as had the local theatre. Whichever football team you supported or from what ever walk of life you came, it was unlikely that you wouldn't find something of interest at the Village that evening.

The chimes of "Going, going, gone . . ." rang out many times as Bryan alternated with local radio disc jockey, Rob Chandler, as celebrity auctioneer. However, by the time the auction had come to an end and the crowd had gone home, Bryan was already bidding for even greater success.

Somebody had successfully bid for four tickets to the gala performance of 'An Evening With Gary Lineker', Bryan's next challenge was about to begin – providing a show to go with the tickets.

A Piece of Fun or The Kiss of Death

Each Friday throughout the 1993/4 football season the Eastern Evening News published a column entitled 'Bryan's Bet' featuring Bryan's tip for the best football bet of the weekend.

When the idea of the bet was first suggested it was intended to serve as a piece of fun which would also help swell the coffers of Bryan's leukaemia appeal.

The Evening News agreed to print the column each week whilst Bookmakers, Coral, provided Bryan with a weekly £10 stake. All winnings from the bets would be credited to the appeal fund with all losing stakes also being returned. With almost 40 bets being anticipated the fund was guaranteed £400 before the first match of the season kicked off.

Due to betting restrictions imposed by the Football League, Bryan was restricted to selecting the outcome of one match of his choice each week. This meant that his bet had to be either on the correct score, the first goal-scorer or the double result (i.e. what the position would be at half time and full time) for that match.

Predicting the correct score or first goal scorer in a football match was never going to be easy and so it was no great surprise when, after the first ten weeks, Bryan had managed to clock up only two successes. However, when that total failed to increase after a further ten weeks 'Bryan's Bet' began to be seen, by many, as a distinct disadvantage if it happened to tip your team for a win. Rumour had it that Premier League bosses up and down the country were sending out for their copies of the Evening News on a Friday night praying that they wouldn't find their team being napped for success the following day!

Originally it had been intended that 'Bryan's Bet' would concentrate, each week, on Norwich's match. It soon became apparent, however, that this could lead to some embarrassment. Obviously, Bryan would feel obliged to predict success for City each week and, as keeper, it would go against the grain for him to predict any scoreline that indicated goals for the opposition.

Indeed when City's first match of the season was revealed as being at home to reigning champions, Manchester United, Bryan didn't have to think twice about his opening gamble. "We've got a dream start to the season and there's no doubt where I'll be placing my first bet," he said.

Seeking revenge for the previous season's defeat, which had all but snuffed out City's own championship challenge, Bryan went on to predict a 1-0 win for the Canaries.

Unfortunately for both Norwich and Bryan, and the fans who had taken his advice and had a small flutter on his prediction, United left Carrow Road 2-0 winners. Undaunted, Bryan stayed with Norwich for the second Saturday of the season when the Canaries travelled to Elland Road, fortress of Leeds United.

Despite their relatively poor 1992/3 season, Leeds had still maintained the league's best home record for that year. No team looked forward to visiting Leeds and City faced a formidable task that not many thought they would rise to.

However, having enjoyed a 3-2 victory over Blackburn Rovers at Ewood Park mid-week, Bryan was confident of another Norwich success. Choosing not to predict a score-line for this match, (a shame as the odds for City's 4-0 win were 100-1), Bryan decided, instead, to try tipping the first goal scorer.

Mark Robins was the man who got the nod as Bryan explained, "Anybody who's seen Robbo banging the ball around in training will know that he's at his sharp shooting best and it's only bad luck that's kept him off the score-sheet so far this season." Words of confidence intended at firing Mark up and, indeed, had you known before the kick-off that City would come away with a 4-0 victory, then you would have thought that the bet had every chance of being successful.

However, it was during the Leeds match that 'Bryan's Bet' assumed the mantle of 'Kiss of Death'. Poor old Robbo did everything in the game except score. Twice he began his celebrations at putting the ball in the back of the net only to see both efforts wiped out by offside decisions. Following those up with a shot against the woodwork he then saw two further goal bound efforts pushed out by Leeds keeper, John Lukic, for Ruel Fox and Chris Sutton to follow up and slot home one each.

Whilst the 4-0 victory ensured euphoria on the coach ride home, Mark Robins had cause to believe that Lady Luck had turned her back on him that afternoon. A quiet word in Bryan's ear that the next time he wanted to express his confidence in his goal-scoring powers, then perhaps he could do it in private, seemed the order of the day.

"O.K. Gaffer, next week I'll bet on Arsenal."

The local derby moves to the local bowling alley.

A Double Strike

Back at the start of the football season, Bryan was persuaded to organise a ten pin bowling match for his leukaemia appeal. After a brief meeting with his fellow City players he quickly came up with a team consisting of Chris Sutton, Mark Robins, Ruel Fox and Rob Newman. Realising that his own greatest claim to bowling was that of 'bowling over' opposing attackers in his eighteen yard box, Bryan decided to act as non-playing captain and threw out a challenge for suitable opposition.

It wasn't too long before the challenge was taken up by the players from Portman Road, and an Ipswich team including striker Chris Kiwomya and goalkeeper Craig Forrest was set to take on the City boys at the Norwich Solar Bowl. The night that the match took place found both teams riding high in the Premier League. City had bounced back from their opening day defeat by Manchester United with successive away wins at Blackburn and Leeds. Ipswich had gone one better by winning all three of their opening matches. The atmosphere was added to by the forthcoming clash between the two teams, at Carrow Road, two days later. Ipswich had been the only team, other than Manchester United, to beat the Canaries at home in the Premier League the previous year and the talk of revenge was in the air.

After the seemingly never-ending session of photographs and autographs was finally over the action began. It soon became apparent that the City team were in no mood to take prisoners and, in no time at all, the Ipswich lads were well and truly trounced. Far from being downhearted the Ipswich players joined Bryan's team for a chat and a few drinks when the game was over. Talk turned, inevitably, to football and a lot of good-natured banter about the Wednesday night game followed. As the Ipswich players rose to leave, Bryan called over to Chris Kiwomya, "I'll see you on Wednesday," he said. Chris grinned broadly and replied, "That's right. Somewhere in the six yard box!"

True to his word, when Wednesday night came, Chris involved Bryan in a series of tussles. He could do nothing, however, to stop City from winning 1-0 and inflicting a double defeat, over their local rivals, in the space of 48 hours.

"You were offside anyway, Chris."

An Evening With Who?

Probably the most ambitious event organised for Bryan's appeal was the adaptation of the stage play 'An Evening With Gary Lineker'. Ambitious, it may have been, but it also proved to be one of the most successful. Staged at the Theatre Royal, Norwich, its success was a testament to all the hard work put into its organisation by everyone involved with it. The list of people was endless, from Bryan himself, together with his co-stars, right through to the theatre staff, all of whom worked free of charge, ensuring that the production would raise as much money as possible.

The clamour for tickets started as soon as the event was announced and 'sold out' notices were being anticipated within days of the box office opening. Excitement grew as the list of both stage and sporting celebrities who would take part grew almost daily. Bryan, of course, was to star in the lead role of Gary Lineker, whilst the well respected actress Samantha Beckinsale would be playing the leading lady.

Rehearsals were arduous and intense as Bryan was forced to practice, over and again, how to kiss Samantha and sweep her off her feet at the end of the play. It may have looked like fun to the casual onlooker, but Bryan assured anybody who would listen that this was, in fact, serious work! Whilst Bryan may have felt the need to rehearse his character, some other roles came more naturally. Ian Culverhouse, for example, took to his part like a duck to water. Wearing a City shirt under his sleeveless jacket, 'Civvy' waltzed around the stage with a broom in his hand as though he'd been a sweeper all his life - and not just since the start of the season.

As the theatre filled up, expectation was high and the

audience sat down to await the start of what promised to be the evening of a lifetime. However, they didn't have to wait for the curtain to go up before the fun started.

It is unlikely that the theatre will ever again be able to call upon so many sporting and acting personalities to act as programme sellers. Members of the cast, together with City players, roamed the auditorium busily signing and selling souvenir programmes to anyone and everyone. Indeed, it would have been a brave person who left the theatre without buying one. Mark Robins, in particular, proved to be as adept at putting programmes into people's hands as he is at putting footballs into the back of the net. If, when his football career comes to an end, he's ever looking for a new trade, then he should have a guaranteed future to look forward to as a newspaper vendor!

Programmes duly bought and read, the good humoured audience settled down to enjoy the show, but there was still another twist to come. Just when they might have been forgiven for believing that all the cast were firmly located backstage, the audience were confronted by more pandemonium in the stalls.

As if from nowhere, a worried looking John Fashanu scrambled along the front rows looking like a fox desperately trying to escape its hunters. Close behind him, cheque book in one hand and fountain pen in the other, ran City chairman, Robert Chase, accompanied by manager Mike Walker clutching a contract for 'Fash the Bash' to sign.

John had, of course, played an important part in the previous day's game at Carrow Road when Wimbledon had beaten City 1-0 and the irony was not lost upon the audience. Like a recurring bad dream, Chase and Walker pursued Fash throughout the play. Every time John appeared on stage you knew the City management team would be close behind. As somebody remarked later, this was the first public appearance of the chairman's cheque book of the season!

Whilst the most obvious, the Fashanu chase was only one of a number of changes made to the play to allow extra people to appear on stage. For sheer farce it would be hard to beat the one which saw the entire City team emerge from a small toilet on stage in what could only be described as theatre comedy at its very best.

As one sporting personality followed another onto the stage, the audience must have felt as if they were watching the numbers board from 'A Question Of Sport'. A special hand was given to ex-Canary star, Andy Linighan, who's last minute goal against Sheffield Wednesday in the F.A. Cup Final had assured City of their first season in Europe. But, naturally enough, the biggest cheer of the night was reserved for Bryan when he walked on stage wearing his kilt and Gary Lineker's number ten England shirt. If ever the house was going to be brought down, then this was the moment.

Admitting to more nerves than when playing for his national team, Bryan had relaxed backstage by watching the live football match between Liverpool and Blackburn on television with John Fashanu. The applause from the audience obviously overwhelmed him, but must have also reassured him that any acting limitations would soon be forgiven.

In the event, both Bryan and his fellow cast members, more used to performing on grass than on 'the boards', played their parts so well that, at times, it was difficult to separate the amateurs from the professionals. Indeed, at the end of the play, when Bryan had to kiss Samantha and sweep her off her feet, he proved that all the hard work of those back-stage rehearsals had really paid off.

The play over and the applause finally dying down, Bryan announced that the evening would end with the drawing of the raffle. One person who had been keen to take part in the evening had been Ian Botham, but other commitments had kept him away. Instead he had sent a signed bat which was the star raffle prize. When Graham Thompson was drawn as the winner he generously offered it back for auction. A £1,000 bid by the City players, led by Rob Newman, soon sealed its fate and another £300 for the Gary Lineker shirt meant that the evening had raised over £30,000 pushing the appeal to over £80,000.

A few weeks before the show, Arthur Smith, the author of 'An Evening With Gary Lineker', had appeared on the Channel 4 chat show, 'Clive Anderson Talks Back'. He

Above: Bryan and Samantha backstage – practice makes perfect.

Below: Here they come again – Chase and Walker on the trail of John Fashanu.

Above: Sweeper 'Civvy' Culverhouse in his usual position.

Below: Bryan and Fash the Bash - sharing the same colours for once.

commented that it wouldn't be possible to write such a play now as the great characters of sport, like Ian Botham and Gary Lineker, had gone. Had he been in the audience that night he might well have changed his mind. For one night only his greatest writing achievement had been given a new title – 'An Evening With Bryan Gunn'.

Bryan, Susan and Melissa celebrate breaking the £100,000 barrier.

The Shutout

As a goalkeeper, Bryan's main objective on the pitch is to keep out the opposition. However, one night he found the boot firmly placed on the other foot.

Playing away at Bradford, in the second round of the Coca Cola Cup, Bryan discovered that it was the opposition who seemed intent on keeping him out.

In the dressing room, shortly before the kick-off, he realised that he had left some things on the team coach outside and a quick trip to retrieve them followed. However, when he made his way back to the players' entrance the steward failed to recognise him and refused to let him back in. Despite his assurances that he was due to be standing between the posts in less than half an hour, the steward wouldn't budge. Thoughts of Mike Walker pulling on the old green jersey must have been giving Bryan nightmares when, fortunately, a group of supporters, passing by, confirmed his identity. Luckily, Bryan made it back to the dressing room just in time to stop the Gaffer from trying on his boots for size!

When Bradford went two goals up, Bryan might have been forgiven for believing that his shutout had been an omen. However, a late goal by Foxy and three goals in five minutes back at Carrow Road, in the second leg, saw City safely through to the next round.

Still, the experience must have given Bryan a whole new meaning for the expression - 'Keeping out the opposition'.

"Yeah and I'm Bruce Grobbelaar, now where's your ticket?"

£100,000 - Off to a Tee

Most professional footballers like to relax with a game of golf, so it wasn't hard for Bryan to put together what, for many people, turned out to be the sporting highlight of his appeal. Finding players prepared to take part in his golf tournament at Sprowston Park, last October, wasn't difficult and, in much the same way that the excitement had built up a few weeks earlier for the celebrity version of 'An Evening With Gary Lineker', so it did again as the list of footballing celebrities due to play was revealed.

Many of the City squad, including Jeremy Goss, Ian Culverhouse and Gary Megson were taking part, as was the management team of Mike Walker and Dixie Deehan. Other players included Phil Neal and Micky Hazard, whilst a strong Arsenal presence was felt via David Seaman, Andy Linighan and Lee Dixon.

As the day dawned the first panic was caused by the news that fellow goalkeepers Bruce Grobbelaar and Chris Woods were unable to play through injuries they had picked up the previous day. The situation worsened when another phone call reporting Dean Saunders unfit to play came through. Despite frantic phone calls, Bryan found he was still one celebrity player short until Phil Neal generously volunteered to go round twice. Such heroism ensured that all 31 teams taking part would be suitably accompanied by a footballing personality, and that Phil would have a very tired arm by the end of the day.

Earlier forecasts in the week of wind and rain had caused a few apprehensive faces to peer out of their bedroom windows that morning, but after an early mist had lifted the day proved to be perfect for a round of golf.

Arriving to a never-ending breakfast, teams were able to meet up with their celebrity player before teeing off. As golfers who wanted to be footballers mixed with footballers who wanted to be golfers, a jovial atmosphere engulfed the breakfast room and everyone looked forward to the day ahead.

The first team to tee off were the Susan Gunn All Stars accompanied by Phil Neal, on his first round of the day. Bryan led the Duffy and McGovern team and went off last, allowing him to welcome all the other teams as they arrived at the first tee. By the time Bryan came to tee off himself, he must have shaken more than enough hands to cause him some concern about the quality of his own swing.

The concept of taking part being as important as winning soon became apparent as Mike Walker sent his first ball flying out of bounds. Continually causing some 'ducking and diving' as he completed his 18 holes. Mike excelled himself on the fairway to the 12th hole where he succeeded in hitting almost every tree. Indeed, so impressed were the course officials at the number of trees he hit, that a special bottle of champagne was presented to Mike later that evening together with an invitation to return the following week to try again for those that he had missed.

Eventually, it came to Bryan's turn to tee off, and there were one or two surprises in store. Discovering that his caddy for the day was a life size Postman Pat was the first, but the second was more explosive. With a large crowd gathered to watch his first shot, together with newspaper and television cameras, it was, perhaps, a little unfortunate that Bryan didn't spot freelance photographer, Roger Harris, switching his golf ball. As Bryan delivered a stroke intended to send his first ball soaring high into the clouds, he could only watch in amazement as it exploded about six inches away from the tee. Much laughter followed as Bryan searched for the culprit before checking and re-checking his next ball.

As the players finished their rounds, they found that the never-ending breakfast had been replaced by a never-ending lunch, over which old golfing stories could be exchanged. After the final lunch had been eaten it was time for the evening's festivities of prize giving and speeches.

Bryan tees off . . . .

. . . . and gets more than he expected!

However, before these started Bryan announced that he had one more surprise in store. Disappearing for a few minutes, he shuffled back into the Bar Room followed by David Seaman, John Polston, Ian Crook, Ian Culverhouse and Lee Dixon. The six players had donned football shirts and Bryan explained that he had a special message for the press who had gathered. The day's golfing had taken his appeal fund through the £100,000 barrier and, when they turned round, the six players revealed that the numbers on the backs of their shirts spelt out 100000.

To tumultuous applause, the cameras started to click and, eager to get the best possible photograph for the next day's paper, the local photographer had the players alternating between twisting, turning, squatting and standing. After watching his players squat down for the sixth or seventh time the voice of Mike Walker could be overhead. "This isn't doing their legs any good. Doesn't he know they've got a match on Wednesday?".

With the photo session over, the prize-giving began. Most players were happy to accept their trophies with a simple thank you, until Andy Linighan took the floor. Treating the audience to a monologue to rival those of Les Dawson, he had his fellow players in stitches as he recalled his own version of the transfer that took him away from Carrow Road.

The only slight disappointment of the day was that no-one had scored a hole in one. Corals had guaranteed a £5,000 bonus to the fund if anybody had succeeded in making the magic shot, but, compared to the overall success of the day, this was a minor upset.

By the time the evening came to an end, 93 golfers had enjoyed the round of a lifetime and the appeal had passed another milestone. Just after midnight Bryan and Susan left the course tired, but satisfied, that they had now raised over £100,000 in the space of just six months. The next target was anybody's guess.

And in the Green and Yellow Corner

The increase in television coverage of football, each year, has the average fan rubbing his hands with glee. To the player, however, the opportunity to constantly repeat and analyse certain moments of a match can prove to be a bit embarrassing.

One such occasion was the second leg of City's UEFA Cup Match away to Vitesse Arnhem of Holland. Struggling to pull back a 3-0 deficit the home team became increasingly frustrated at being unable to break down City's defence. At one point, as tempers threatened to flare, Bryan found himself almost 40 yards from his goal helping to defuse what could have turned into an ugly moment. Unfortunately, a few minutes later the cameras picked up Bryan having a less than complimentary conversation with an Arnhem attacker who had just tried to take a large chunk out of his leg. How much English the Dutchman spoke is unknown, but it is unlikely that he didn't understand the general meaning of Bryan's comments or the consequences of another similar tackle.

The Friday of the same week was the so-called 'Battle of Britain' fight between Lennox Lewis and Frank Bruno. Such was the way that the cameras had picked up Bryan's own altercation that it was being whispered that Barry Hearn was considering inviting Bryan down to Cardiff Arms Park as first reserve.

Thankfully, in football, a difference of opinion is usually all over within a few minutes, rather than in a few rounds. However, should Lennox or Frank ever decide to take up football for a living, they may well find that the area around Bryan's goal is one ring they wouldn't have automatic control over.

"Any more nonsense and I'm bringing in Bryan!"

Bayern Munich – Parts One and Two
(And Introducing The Green Flash)

After the success over Vitesse Arnhem, everybody at Carrow Road was hoping for a plum tie in the second round of the UEFA Cup. The victory over the Dutch team had been emphatic, but there were still the doubters who wondered how City would cope against 'real' European opposition.

The fact that Vitesse were a seeded team counted for nothing. Relatively unknown in this country, they were still regarded as a somewhat part-time club, who had only made the cup in the first place because the standards in Holland were so low. Needless to say this was not a view shared by the City team, and they were all keen to set the record straight in the next round.

Sure enough, when the draw was made, the Canaries got the result they wanted. If the name Vitesse Arnhem meant little in the footballing world, then that of Bayern Munich couldn't be overstated. Drawn to play away in the first leg, City had come out of the hat smiling.

For the next couple of weeks, all football talk in Norwich was of how the Canaries would fare in the Olympic Stadium. The task was formidable, few English teams had ever come away from Munich with a draw and none had ever come home as winners. It was generally accepted that Bryan and his defence would be in for a testing evening.

However, when the big night finally arrived things didn't go exactly to plan. Far from being forced back into their own area, it was the Canaries who took the match by the scruff of the neck and threatened to steamroll the mighty Bayern Munich right out of Europe.

'Gunny' and 'Gossy' celebrate their victory over Bayern Munich.

Much to the amazement of the mainly German crowd, City were soon a goal up thanks to the 'man of the moment', Jeremy Goss. However, if the Germans expected the Canaries to sit back and protect this lead, they were in for an even bigger shock. Totally dominating the first half, City threatened to increase their lead with every attack, and it came as no great surprise when Mark Bowen slipped in behind the Munich defence to turn a 1-0 lead into 2-0. Against the run of play, moments before half time, the Germans pulled a goal back and, as they walked off for the interval, the City team could have been forgiven for wondering if this might be the start to a Munich comeback in the second half.

However, when the teams returned to the pitch to continue their battle, little changed. If anything, City dominated even more in the second half than they had in the first. Certainly, if any team was going to score again, it always looked more likely to be the Canaries. At the end of the match the scoreline was the same as it had been at half time. Norwich had become the first English team, ever, to defeat the famous Bayern Munich on their own ground. What would the critics say now?

During the two weeks between the first and second legs, the German newspapers went to war. Norwich was, they explained, a small village in the east of England where everyone worked on the fields and ate mustard. The German giants would have no trouble in retrieving the match in the second leg. Bayern star, Lothar Matthaus, was quoted as describing Norwich as "a very ordinary side". And so the scene was set for the mighty Germans to face, once more, this 'very ordinary side' at Carrow Road. It was a game that Bryan was later to describe as his 'greatest ever match'.

The game took place two nights before Guy Fawkes and the City crowd were hoping for some early fireworks. They weren't to be disappointed, although the first blast was definitely the sort of rocket they could have done without. Only four minutes into the match, the Germans grabbed the early goal they so desperately wanted and the pressure was suddenly very much on City. Probably sensing they were needed, the Carrow Road crowd reacted admirably. The cheering and singing around the ground would have misled any late comers into believing it was the Canaries who had taken the lead.

Showing far more flair and imagination than they had at home, the Germans began to put some good moves together. Twice they threatened to take an aggregate lead, but twice they were foiled by Bryan as he reacted superbly with world-class saves from Christian Ziege and Alphonso Valencia. But the moment of the match was still to come. Shaking off his defender, for once, Jeremy Goss suddenly found himself free to fire the ball into the back of the Bayern net. Carrow Road erupted and, although there were no fireworks in the crowd, a green streamer had exploded on the pitch. Racing past an astonished defence and an open mouthed management team, Bryan covered the entire length of the pitch to reward Gossy with a massive bear-hug in the Bayern area. The look on Jeremy's face gave the impression that even if it hadn't been scripted, the occasion wasn't totally unexpected.

The goal gave City back their grip on the match and, the longer the game went on, the more likely they looked to be the team who would increase their goal tally. Tension rose as the seconds ticked away until, a couple of minutes before full time, Lothar Matthaus found himself in Bryan's six yard box arguing with the referee. A few words of advice from Bryan weren't taken too kindly and, following a quick shoving match, Bryan found himself facing his first European yellow card.

With the end of the game came the start of the celebrations. Norwich had now proven their European pedigree once and for all. On a night that had seen both Manchester United and Aston Villa crash out of Europe, the Canaries were keeping the English flag flying high. An added bonus for Bryan was the fact that Gossy's goal had put another £425 into his leukaemia appeal as a result of a free bet he had been given by Coral. Perhaps that's why Bryan had made his long run that night, being in the opponent's area certainly wasn't one of Mike Walker's tactics. I wonder what odds he would have got on that.

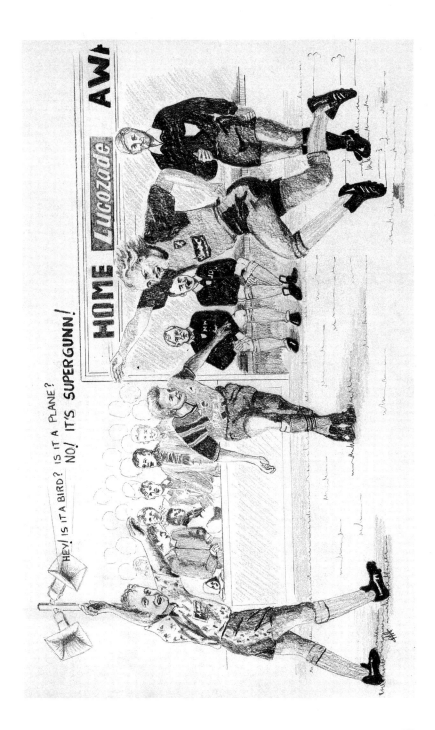

The Question

It's that age-old question that every husband gets asked at some stage of his marriage by his wife: "So where were you when I needed you?"

Sometimes it's asked rhetorically, sometimes sarcastically and sometimes accusingly, but never with the desire of gaining information. Indeed, the answer to the question is invariably known before it is asked and the sole point of asking it is simply to create a feeling of guilt.

Irrespective of the answer, one thing is undeniable - you certainly weren't where you should have been.

So when the floods came last year and Susan was busy bailing out the Gunn household, where exactly were you Bryan? Playing football with your Scottish mates in Italy? Surely not!

"No dear, it's been quite sunny actually."

A Date To Remember

It's not unusual to hear people remark on how famous moments in time stand out in their memories. It's as if that precise second has been frozen in their minds forever and has become part of their own history.

For many people it's the assassination of John F. Kennedy, with millions throughout the world still able to recall every detail of where they were and what they were doing at the very moment they heard of his shooting on that awful day in November 1963. For Bryan, no doubt, the most important moment of 1963,was exactly one month later when he was born.

One moment likely to stand out in Bryan's memory, however, is the coach ride to Sheffield on Friday, November 5th last year. The Canaries were playing away at Sheffield United the following day, but that wasn't what made the trip so memorable. Guy Fawkes night it may well have been, but it didn't take fireworks to light up the coach that night.

Mid-way through the journey, as they travelled up the M1, all ears on the coach were firmly glued to the radio. The draw for the third round of the UEFA Cup was being made and City were eagerly awaiting to find out what their reward for beating Bayern Munich in the previous round would be.

Everyone was hoping for a big team and they weren't to be disappointed as the name of Inter Milan came out of the hat as their next opponents.

"The whole coach cheered," said Ian Culverhouse later, "we just erupted when we heard the draw". The players' feelings were echoed by the management team.

"We're delighted with the draw," confirmed Mike Walker, with John Deehan adding, "the players are all excited at the thought of taking on one of the biggest names in world football".

Away from the coach it wasn't just the players and management who were thrilled at the prospect of bringing mighty Inter Milan to Carrow Road. Thoughts of travelling to the magnificent San Siro stadium for the second leg, a fortnight later, made the hairs stand up on the back of many a City supporter's neck. Celebrations continued long into the night as plans for an Italian invasion began to take shape.

Equally pleased were the BBC who had bought the rights to cover all City's UEFA Cup home games. Another Sportsnight 'Live Special' was immediately announced and the nation eagerly looked forward to the next chapter in City's amazing European adventure. Indeed, the only person who seemed disappointed with the draw was Inter coach, Osvaldo Bagnoli, who admitted, "I would have hoped for an easier opponent". That remark, alone, bore witness to the new found respect Norwich were now commanding in Europe.

And so it was that an excited coach load of players continued their journey up the M1 towards Sheffield. The chance to play against world stars like Dennis Bergkamp, Ruben Rosa and Igor Shalimov in the 75,000 seater San Siro was enough to ensure that the date would be firmly fixed in everyone's memories. And, despite rumours to the contrary, I am certain that these were the reasons why Bryan would remember that date so vividly.

The fact that the players had organised a sweepstake on who their next opponents in Europe would be, had nothing to do with it. And the fact that Bryan had won it meant even less. "Money goes to money," was Ian Culverhouse's other quote. He didn't say if the coach was still cheering when they found out who had the winning ticket.

"Yeah it's a great draw, Gaffer, but can you remember who's holding the sweepstake kitty?"

The Ups and Downs of European Football

Above: Success at Arnham

Below: Only disappointment in the San Siro.

A Little Bit Of French

A constant factor of City's play last season was the quality of their football. From keeper to striker the players were constantly applauded by the critics for the level of their skills and the calibre of their play.

Every player received his own accolades but Bryan, in particular, was often singled out for special praise. His saves in the League, Cup and European matches often left the critics open-mouthed whilst his opponents could only shake their heads in disbelief.

Whilst Bryan's acrobatics between the posts were a major factor in City's continuing success it was only one facet of a team capable of, and committed to, playing football as a spectator sport. No doubt it was reassuring to the team to be constantly touted as an example of football excellence, but it must have also been somewhat galling to see the media continue to temper that praise with a little surprise. After all, Norwich were only carrying on the traditions and standards they had set themselves the previous season.

One match in particular that caught the public imagination was City's game against Manchester United at Old Trafford early last December. A record 23 countries were receiving the game live by satellite and they were, no doubt, anticipating another professional United performance to strengthen their stranglehold at the top of the Premier League. After all, City were playing the 2nd leg of their UEFA Cup match against Inter Milan at the famous San Siro stadium only 4 days later and would, surely, have one eye on that match.

However, to the surprise of many, it was City who took the match by the scruff of its neck and for the first 30 minutes

United must have wondered what had hit them. Totally dominated by a rampant City strike force they were lucky not to find themselves 3 or 4 goals down in the first 20 minutes or so. To the neutral supporters in any of those 23 countries watching, it must have seemed as if the league positions had been mixed up somewhere in the translation as Norwich played more like the team who were sitting 10 points clear at the top of the league. Bryan's greatest problem in that opening half hour must have been keeping warm and when, after a flash of genius by Ryan Giggs on 30 minutes, he found himself picking the ball out of the back of the net he would have been justified to feel more than a little unlucky. Still, far from being disheartened, City roared back from the kick-off and were level within a minute when Chris Sutton fired home a beauty from 25 yards.

That goal seemed to open the floodgates for a feast of attacking football. The final 60 minutes was more like a tennis match than a football one as the ball seemed to travel from end to end quicker than it did in the days of those McEnroe-Connors epics. It seemed one minute Bryan would be saving at the feet of Hughes or Giggs, when the next would see Foxy bringing out the best from Schmeichel at the other end.

The 23 countries watching must have wondered how it was, with such good football still being played in Britain's Premier League, that none of the four home countries had qualified for the World Cup finals.

A final scoreline of 2-2 seemed to keep everybody happy. It was a game that both sides probably felt they could have nicked but equally it was a game that neither side really deserved to lose.

Man of the match for United was Eric Cantona who displayed all the skills and genius people had come to expect from him. He was involved in both United goals and looked a danger every time he got into the box.

Half-volleys, snap-shots, headers and dummies had all failed to beat Bryan when, towards the end, a delicate lob looked certain to finally put Cantona on the scoresheet. However, a last second push over by Bryan brought howls of approval from the travelling Canary fans and gasps of disbelief from the home crowd. At this point it must have become apparent to Eric that he was not going to beat Bryan on this particular afternoon. With a friendly wave he called over, "Tres bien, Le Gardien".

Bryan didn't need an interpreter to understand the sentiment and a quick grin spoke volumes. All the press accolades in the world are nice to have but nothing beats a genuine compliment from a fellow professional. Bryan may well have been tempted to reply, "Merci, Monsieur," but, no doubt, thought better of it. After all he wouldn't have wanted his defence to think he was pleading for help!

"Merci, Monsieur."
"Don't worry Bryan, we'll look after you".

Finders Keepers

The old saying, "You can't make a silk purse from a sow's ear," has been proven to be true time and time again over the years. In much the same way, it is generally accepted that any team is only as good as the parts that make it up. Try imagining, for example, The Beatles without John Lennon, Torville without Dean or fish without chips, and you'll begin to get the picture.

Similarly, the same applies to any successful football team, with that success depending on a strong defence, a creative midfield and an opportunist forward line all rolled into one. Each position is of equal importance and by removing any one, you weaken the whole.

However, to the youngster with dreams of embarking on a football career, the two most attractive positions have long been those of goalkeeper and centre forward. Not too surprising, perhaps, when you consider that most games are decided by the number of goals scored. With the centre forward's main aim being to put the ball into the back of the net, whilst the goalkeeper's job is to keep it out, it is often the case that games are won and lost by the performance of these two players and, therefore, an extra glamour factor is attached to the respective positions.

There are few more thrilling sights in a football match than that of the centre forward breaking free and getting into a one-on-one situation with the opposing goalkeeper. A battle of wits follows as the centre forward tries to disguise his intentions whilst the keeper attempts to outguess him. There can only be one winner in each encounter and these tend to be the moments remembered when the match is over. Certainly, in

City's case, the media and fans have tended to follow this attitude, with Bryan and Chris Sutton picking up over half of the 'Man of the Match' awards of the season between them.

However, there may be some goalkeepers who feel that when the two roles are appraised they are, sometimes, treated somewhat differently. Take, for a moment, the following example. A gifted centre forward gets seven clear cut chances each week for six weeks. He misses four each week but manages to convert the other three. Six weeks later, with six hat tricks under his belt and six match balls sitting proudly at home, he is the pride and joy of his club. The fans adore him, the media are promoting him as the greatest goal scorer of all time and he's on his way to a permanent place in his national team.

Now turn the example upside down. A similarly gifted goalkeeper is also faced with seven clear cut chances each week for six weeks. He achieves exactly the same ratio as the star centre forward, pulling off three world-class saves and letting in the other four. Six weeks later he's let in twenty-four goals, the fans are on his back, the media are calling him Cinderella (always late for the ball!) or worse, and the only place he's going is into the reserves. In theory both players have performed to an identical standard, yet one is a national hero whilst the other is the local villain.

It shouldn't be too surprising, then, that more and more schoolboys, aiming to be footballing stars of the future, are turning their backs on the goalkeeping role and looking, instead, to the centre forward position as their passport to fame. And, if you don't believe me, take a look at the current Premiership line up of goalkeepers and try spotting the Englishman.

As Scotland's number one keeper, Bryan is a member of the fastest growing club in English football - the foreign goalkeeper's society. Who would have believed, ten or twenty years ago, that we would have to go searching abroad for goalkeepers to defend our top teams. It was an unwritten law, in the days of Banks, Shilton, Clemmence and Bonnetti, that, as far as goalkeepers went, English meant 'best'. Most foreign keepers were treated with a certain amount of scorn and you were always confident that you would score goals against them. The name of Grobbelaar stood out like a lone beacon in the First Division when English keepers ruled supreme, but how that has all changed.

Names like Schmeichel, Thorsvelt and Bosnich stand out for United, Spurs and Villa. At Leeds there is Lukic, at Chelsea you'll find Kharine, Miklosko stars for West Ham, Stejskal rules at Q.P.R. and Segers is part of the Wimbledon 'crazy gang'. Ogrizovic has been sent to Coventry and Srnicek has taken the coals to Newcastle. Add to that, Republic of Ireland's Kelly at Sheffield United and Welsh star Southall at Everton, whilst not forgetting big Canadian Craig Forrest at Ipswich, and you go some way to explaining why Bryan and his non-English colleagues are making the Premier League look like a subsidiary of the League of Nations.

Gone are the days when we used to smile as the Welsh and Irish national teams had to search in the lower divisions for their keepers. Gone too is the intense competition for the England Number One jersey. Can it really be possible that should David Seaman of Arsenal and Blackburn's Tim Flowers ever get injured at the same time that we could see Terry Venables making the same searches?

If, as the media and fans demand, the game is to become more attack orientated, then it follows that goalkeepers will be spending more time picking the ball out of the net. Far from lampooning this development we should be applauding them for the ones that they are keeping out. When a commentator remarks, at the end of a game finishing 3-3, that it could have been eight each, then we should remember the five that the keeper saved as much as the three that he let in. If we're not careful we may end up with no-one competing for the Number One jersey at all.

"It's O.K. lads, I hear Arsenal are still using an English guy!"

It's That Man Again

All leading sports personalities are bound to attract media attention from time to time. Performing on an island as sports orientated as Britain mean success and exposure are guaranteed to go hand in hand.

Every now and again a personality will come along who appears to dominate his or her chosen sport. What George Best and Gazza did for football, Ian Botham and Geoffrey Boycott did for cricket. With boxing it was Muhammed Ali and, more recently Frank Bruno, whilst Lester Piggott and Willie Carson have kept a high profile for racing. Other names like Nigel Mansell, Steve Davis, Sebastian Coe and Torville and Dean have ensured that all sports have had their leading players.

However, as far as the Norwich newspapers were concerned, in 1993 the name of Bryan Gunn outshone them all. When it came to attracting media coverage Bryan could have given lessons to Michael Jackson.

Kicking off his leukaemia appeal, towards the end of the 1992/3 football season, Bryan let it be known that he would be available to the local press, radio and television at practically any time of the day or night. He realised that the appeal would be far more successful with media support and to that end all but forfeited his own private life.

From the day the appeal was launched Bryan was rarely out of the public eye. Attending dinners, opening shops and conducting autograph sessions became a way of life as he toured up and down the county to accept cheques and donations from anybody who had gone to the trouble of raising funds.

When it was announced that Bryan was intending to take more of a back seat role in the campaign many people treated

Taking a break for lunch - and the fans soon join in.

the announcement with a certain amount of scepticism. The appeal had become synonymous with Bryan's name and it seemed unlikely that he would be able to let go of it just like that.

The date Bryan gave for his last engagement was October 31st and, sure enough, there he was again, just one day later on November 1st, attending a Coral shop opening in Dereham with Jeremy Goss. The very same evening saw him teaming up with Chris Sutton, Efan Ekoku and Ruel Fox to act as a waiter at the Pizza Parlour in Norwich.

Both events were guaranteed to put yet more money into his appeal fund. Pizza Parlour were donating 70% of their evenings turnover to the appeal, whilst Coral had given Jeremy a free £50 bet on himself to score the first goal in the second leg of the UEFA Cup match against Bayern Munich a couple of days later. If the bet was successful Coral would pay another £850 to the appeal, whilst if it should lose they would still donate the £50 stake.

In the event, Jeremy didn't score the first goal but he did grab the equaliser which saw the Canaries win the match by an aggregate score of 3-2. In the circumstances, big hearted bookies, Coral, handed over half the winnings - £425 - to the appeal. All in all not a bad result from a day's work undertaken 24 hours after the official deadline of 31st October had passed.

During the summer and autumn months of 1993 it seemed almost impossible to open the local newspapers without seeing either a picture of Bryan or an article on his appeal. In fact one school was, reportedly, toying with the idea of running a competition to find a copy of the local Evening News without a picture of Bryan included. No doubt a photo of Bryan presenting the prize would have appeared in the next day's edition! In the end, the school decided to go for something a bit easier - like simultaneously rearranging a dozen Rubik cubes whilst repeating the Greek alphabet backwards.

Apart from the newspaper coverage, Bryan was also to be seen more and more on television. Programmes such as 'Match of the Day' and 'Sportsnight' featured Bryan and Norwich City as a matter of course with City's distinctive style of play earning

Bryan on 'A Question Of Sport'.

them more appearances than ever before. Sky Sports were also jumping on the bandwagon eagerly persuing Bryan and the Canaries as far away as Munich together with regular Sunday afternoon and Monday night specials.

Many readers will recall Bryan's appearance on 'A Question Of Sport' where he correctly over-ruled team captain, Ian Botham, on the picture board whilst helping his team to a resounding victory. Oh, and did anybody else spot him in the audience at the BBC's 'Sports Personality of the Year' programme, sitting next to Mike Walker? In fact Mike remarked later that he and Bryan had been unable to stay and enjoy the disco and buffet afterwards due to having to return home for yet another television spot - the next day's home match against Leeds being shown live on Sky Sports!

As reigning City 'Player of the Year' and PFA representative, together with all the media attention he was receiving, it would have been easy for Bryan to have become 'Mr. Norwich City'. Certainly he was the most instantly recognisable City star - with or without that pony tail. However, Bryan being the person he is, took it all in his stride and, in his own words, 'got on with the job'.

But it wasn't just in Norwich where Bryan's fame grew. Indeed, rumour has it that when Norwich travelled to Italy for the second leg of their UEFA Cup tie against Inter Milan, Bryan was invited by the Vatican to join the Pope on the balcony at St. Peter's Square. Apparently when they came out together, to the roar of approval from the million or so visitors, a young boy at the back of the crowd nudged his dad and asked, "Hey dad, who's that up there with Bryan?"

"Hey dad, who's that man up there with Bryan?"

Inter The Unknown

When the draw for the third round of the UEFA cup matched City against Italian giants, Inter Milan, the local media machine went into overdrive. Whilst City's pairing with Bayern Munich in the previous round had been a great step forward, this draw took them a colossal leap further. Bayern Munich were big but, when it came to European Goliaths, Inter Milan were one of the mightiest.

Excitement was at fever pitch as fans exchanged opinions on how Bryan and the lads would overcome the stars of the Italian, Serie A, league. That they could beat the Italians wasn't in doubt. Not only had they defeated the best that Germany could throw at them in the last round, but they had played them off the park at the same time. The Italians would receive similar treatment and be soundly beaten in the first leg at Carrow Road, a fortnight later. The optimism against Bayern Munich was replaced with confidence against Inter Milan.

Despite some controversy surrounding the ticket sales for the home leg, the atmosphere at Carrow Road, when the two teams took the pitch, was electric. Shown live on the BBC, who must have been congratulating themselves on selecting the Canaries as the only British team they would follow in Europe, the match was guaranteed an audience of several million.

From the kick off City demonstrated that they were prepared to match the Italians in every department. As they forced attack after attack, surely it was only a matter of time before they scored. Inter Milan, on the other hand, had obviously come happy to get a draw, attacking only on the occasional break. Their defence held firm as City flooded their area with wave after wave of attacks.

Jeremy Goss had had his usual £50 wager on scoring the first goal and, when his second half volley crashed against the crossbar, you could almost hear the bookies heading for their wallets.

However, as anybody who watches Serie A football on Channel 4 will know, the Italian defences are amongst the hardest in the world to break down. And so it proved that night at Carrow Road. Despite sustained pressure, Inter held firm and, with just ten minutes to go, they suddenly launched a counter-attack. Most of the City team had been pressing forward and the attack caught the Canaries on the hop. Unable to get back in time, Rob Newman found himself felling Sosa just inside the City box. For a second it seemed as if time had stood still until the referee pointed to the penalty spot.

Not having had that much to do in the match, Bryan now found himself in the unenviable position of having to save the game single-handedly. Dennis Bergkamp, the man who had done so much damage to England's World Cup hopes, was about to strike again. Sending Bryan the wrong way, Bergkamp put the Italians a goal in front and, despite ten frenetic minutes by the city strike force, the score remained the same when the full time whistle was blown. To add insult to injury, the trio of Ians - Culverhouse, Crook and Butterworth - had picked up a booking apiece during the match ensuring their absence from the return leg in the San Siro stadium, a fortnight later. Beaten and bruised, the Canaries left the pitch to lick their wounds.

That the game was over, however, was by no means certain. City had the best away record in the Premier League and had also gone to the Olympic Stadium, Munich, in the previous round and won. It would mean blooding a few more youngsters, in the absence of the three Ians, but nobody accepted that the tie was beyond them.

Certainly the BBC knew there was plenty more excitement to come. A quick discussion around the negotiating table meant that the second leg would also be shown live on T.V. Speculation about City's chances remained high and the BBC added to it with their own advertising campaign. Showing brief highlights of the first leg, interspersed with stills of the City

Above: Bergkamp is kept out by the City defence.

Below: He finaly beats Bryan from the penalty spot.

players, the trailer concluded with a drum roll announcing "The Canaries Secret Weapon - Super Gunn!" If Bryan hadn't felt any pressure up to this point, then the BBC were doing their best to create some.

With the trailers came the announcement that the game would be played in the afternoon and, whilst this would have suited most people on a Saturday or Sunday, with the game being played on a Wednesday, there was immediate uproar. Fearing mass absenteeism, many firms and factories announced they would be closing down for the day. Schools throughout Norfolk made arrangements for football crazy youngsters to watch the match in sports halls, and television sets appeared on shop counters throughout the City overnight.

Even the shopping arrangements of the player's wives had to be altered. Having been originally looking forward to an afternoon in the Italian clothes shops, the girls would now arrive just in time for the match. "Not even enough time to buy a couple of Italian suits," rued Bryan's wife, Susan.

When the day of the match arrived, what seemed like the entire population of Norfolk settled down to see if their team could upset the odds once more. The centre of Norwich became almost a ghost-town as factories ground to a halt and shops put up early closing notices. The market, decked out in yellow and green, saw their trade collapse, and the taxi lads switched off their control radios and tuned in to the sports programme instead.

Out in Milan, the City players waited to take the pitch, eager to restore the status quo. If anybody had doubted City's desire to turn the tie around, all doubts would soon be dispelled. Totally refusing to be overawed by the occasion, the Canaries started where they had left off at Carrow Road a fortnight earlier. It is unlikely that the home crowd had ever witnessed such a one-sided match in their stadium, with their side being on the receiving end. City tore into the heart of the Italian defence from the first whistle. Attack after attack rained down onto the Inter area threatening to bring the score level but, experts at defending when their backs are against the wall, the Italians stood defiant.

In the dying minutes City threw everything they had left at the home team in a last desperate bid for an equaliser. And, just as they had at Carrow Road, the Italians suddenly launched their own counter-attack. Finding themselves outnumbered, the City defence were unable to stop the ball finding its way, once more, to that man Bergkamp. As Bryan came out to narrow the angle, Bergkamp powered a shot into the corner of the net.

Two minutes later it was all over. Despite having had the lion's share of possession, having launched the most attacks and having played the best football in both matches, City had lost both legs 1-0 and were out of Europe. The relief on the mighty Milan faces was there for all to see. They'd had a war on their hands and were happy to have survived it. An aide to Milan coach, Osvaldo Bagnoli, conceded after the match, "Norwich are one of the best teams to have come here in the last ten years, and that includes A.C. Milan, Real Madrid and teams like that".

It didn't alter the result, but it confirmed what everyone already knew. Norwich had gone into Europe and triumphed. The fact that they were out of the UEFA Cup was softened by what they had achieved and how they had performed whilst in it. Norwich had now joined the ranks of the other great British teams who had flown the flag in Europe. And whilst the Super Gunn hadn't quite got them through this time, they would return on another day.

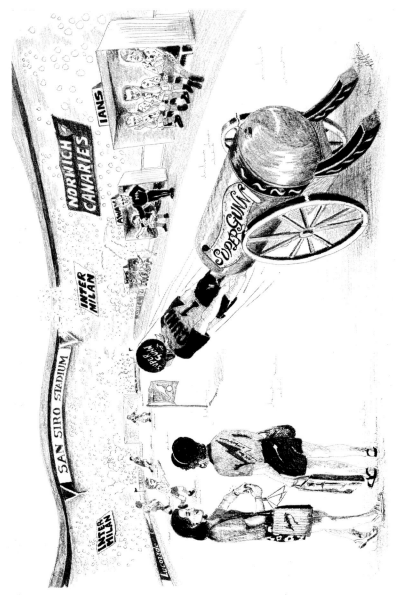

"It's alright for Bryan. All he needs is a new helmet and he's well away."

Bryan and his opposite number, Walter Zenga, in the San Siro Stadium.

Leeds - At The Double

One thing about playing football in England is that you can always rely on the weather to provide you with every permutation. From blistering hot afternoons in August to the freezing hail of a mid-week match in January, the players have to face everything the elements can throw at them.

One match, in particular, that stands out because of the weather conditions was City's home game against Leeds last year. Shown live on Sky, the match was played on Monday, 13th December and, if you were a warm weather supporter, it was certainly unlucky 13 for you.

After torrential rain for most of the day, it was a tribute to the ground staff at Carrow Road that the match took place at all. However, the signs were not good for City. Their last match had seen them knocked out of Europe by Inter Milan and they had won only one of their last eleven games. The popular press was full of speculation that players, such as Chris Sutton and Ruel Fox, would soon be lured away and a connection was being made between boss Mike Walker and the vacancy at Goodison Park.

Injuries hadn't helped them either and they were missing players like John Polston, Ian Butterworth, Ian Crook and Jeremy Goss. On top of that, Leeds were on an unbeaten run of 14 games and were, no doubt, still smarting from the 4-0 drubbing that the Canaries had given them at Elland Road earlier in the season. All in all the prophets of doom were out in force and City were not expected to do well. The bookies had the match as a draw banker and not many people fancied City to win. It was not the best night to run out onto a cold and rain-swept pitch.

The previous evening had seen Bryan in the audience at the BBC's 'Sports Personality of the Year' awards, but the warmth of the television studio must have seemed a million miles away as he waited, with the rest of the team, to brave the arctic conditions.

One thing that would have brightened the evening for Bryan was his meeting with fifteen year old Hayley Johnson shortly before the kick off. Hayley had been diagnosed as having leukaemia when she was five years old and here she was, ten years later, presenting Bryan with a cheque for £650 she had helped to raise, proving conclusively that the research and treatment really did work. For a moment Bryan might have reflected that there were more important things in life than football but, as he stood in the tunnel an hour or so later, his mind would have been only on the game ahead.

When the game started, Bryan would have soon had his worst fears confirmed as the ball skidded around like an elephant on ice-skates. In conditions like those, that night, the worst thing for a keeper is a well hit ball along the ground. He's never really sure if it's going to bounce up or not and the Leeds players certainly tried to catch Bryan out with one or two early on. At the other end, of course, City were trying to do the same and shortly before half-time Chris Sutton latched onto a deft flick from Mark Bowen to side-foot the Canaries into the lead.

Whilst the players would have been delighted to end the first forty-five minutes a goal in front, they would have been under no illusions as they made their way to the dressing room. Leeds were in no mood to roll over, and a testing second half lay ahead. Whilst the fans would be using the interval to visit the soup and tea bars to keep warm, manager Mike Walker was no doubt emphasising that Leeds would be planning to turn up the heat themselves in the second half.

The second half started much the same as the first, with both sets of players attacking the ball in such a manner to suggest that they were as keen to keep warm as the crowd. Just after an hour of the match had gone, Bryan brought off a double save that must have warmed the bones of the Carrow Road faithful. Diving first to his left to block a screamer from Tony Dorigo,

Another game - another Man of the Match award.

he then managed to change direction and push Rod Wallace's follow-up onto the post. However, just five minutes later he was finally beaten by another Wallace effort that slipped in by his left hand post.

The Leeds goal seemed to inspire City more than it did United and suddenly it was Mark Beeney's goal mouth that was under siege. Following sustained pressure, Efan Ekoku finally grabbed the winner for City with ten minutes left to go. Seeing his first shot blocked by the Leed's keeper, 'The Chief' buried the rebound and assured the Canaries of their first league double of the season. Having missed what appeared to be a couple of easier chances earlier on in the game, the goal must have been a welcome confidence booster for Efan, and it sent the Carrow Road crowd wild with ecstacy.

At the end of the game Bryan deservedly received the 'Man of the Match' award, together with the customary bottle of champagne. Leeds own man of the match was, surely, Bryan's fellow Scot, Gordon Strachan, who had tirelessly covered the pitch throughout the game. Bryan and Gordon had been friends for a long time and always enjoyed a friendly, but combative, tussle on the pitch.

Their paths had also crossed recently away from the playing field. A week or so earlier Bryan had been in Manchester for the recording of 'A Question Of Sport' and Gordon was there that day too. The BBC record up the three programmes at a time and Gordon was appearing on the show the week before Bryan. They both partnered Ian Botham, and it was noticeable that the week when Gordon accompanied Ian their team went from being eight points in front to losing the game. The following week Bryan helped Ian to a resounding victory.

It's interesting to note that when Leeds came to Carrow Road they were eight points in front of the Canaries in the Premier League. Under the circumstances, perhaps Bryan and Gordon should have both known the outcome of the game before it started!

"Just the numbers board, lads, then you can have that shower."

Elvis Lives - You Bet!

As 1993 turned into 1994 the winds of change were hard at work at Carrow Road. City manager, Mike Walker, had been linked to Everton for the past two months and, despite repeated assurances from the boardroom, his position remained uneasy.

Eventually, less than a week into the new year, Mike had been installed at Goodison Park, leaving City temporarily without a manager for the forthcoming F.A. Cup tie away to Wycombe Wanderers. John 'Dixie' Deehan was appointed as caretaker manager and received the full support of the City squad with Bryan speaking for everyone when he said, "We're all behind Dixie one hundred per cent. We've looked sharp in training and now just want to get on with the job".

Get on with the job they did and came away from Wycombe with a professional 2-0 win earning them the plum tie in the fourth round - a home draw against Manchester United.

A few days after the Wycombe match Dixie was installed as permanent manager and a few more changes were in store.

"Don't call me 'Dixie'," was the battle cry as John declared that he felt the position of City manager should command a little more respect. Light-heartedly threatening to fine anyone who broke his new rule Dixie ensured that the club carried on with as little turmoil as possible.

One thing that didn't change was novelty bets designed to help raise funds for Bryan's appeal. Corals had come up with a selection of unusual 1994 bets for their customers and had invited the Evening News to choose one and have a free bet on behalf of Bryan's leukaemia fund.

Accordingly, the paper printed the list of choices and invited its readers to vote on which one they felt most appropriate. The selection was wide and varied, and ranged from John Major, Bill Clinton and The Queen all being replaced by the end of the year, to extra-terrestrial life being confirmed on Earth during the next 12 months.

In the end the paper's readers overwhelmingly voted for the money to go on Elvis Presley being found alive before the year's end and the bet was duly placed.

All that was needed now was the return of the 'King of Rock 'n' Roll' and a few thousand pounds more would go into Bryan's ever-increasing fund. Whilst rumours of Elvis being spotted in various chip shops and burger bars persisted throughout the following months, at the time of writing the bet was still waiting to be collected.

Somebody suggested that its best chance of success would be the arrival of a convincing impersonator searching for a new identity, and volunteers were being sought.

"When I said, 'sing Dixie' I was talking about the song."

Above and below: Bryan leads the Canaries away from the Kop after the last game played in front of one of the world's most famous crowds.

It's The Ponytail Kid

" Seldom has so much been written about so little," was the observation of one critic when asked about Bryan's hairstyle. It's unlikely that when Bryan first decided to sport a ponytail, he had any idea of the interest it would generate. Indeed, the subject of Bryan's hair gained almost as much media attention as you would expect that of a major pop star's to.

In a way, that mirrored the position that the Canaries found themselves in, as a club, Bryan was forced to work with limited resources. His imagination, however, was good enough to ensure that he could happily give lessons to both Bobby Charlton and Arthur Scargill on how to make the most of what you've got.

Having allowed his hair to grow to a suitable length, Bryan purchased his first ribbon and, at his charity golf day last October, he unveiled his new secret weapon - The Bryan Gunn Ponytail. Whilst unusual, Bryan's ponytail wasn't unique, and he wasn't the only keeper in the Premier League to have adopted the P.J. Proby look. Bruce Grobbelaar, of Liverpool, had been doing his own impersonation of Basil Brush for some months and, as he was due to play in Bryan's golf tournament that day, speculation about what would happen when the two ponytailed keepers met was high.

As it happened, a message from Bruce, explaining that a strain he had picked up the previous day would prevent him from playing, meant that the clash would not take place. Amidst a few knowing smiles, there were rumours as to whether or not Bruce's injury was genuine, or whether someone had simply informed him that, "this course ain't big enough for two ponytails!" Whichever it was, High Noon at Sprowston Park had been postponed.

Following the golf day, the Bryan Gunn Ponytail was regularly seen around Norwich, both on and off the football pitch. No doubt there was some ribbing in the dressing room, and certainly the press gave it plenty of exposure. Reports started to appear in the local newspapers which would begin, "Ponytailed Bryan Gunn was seen today at . . . ." or "Bryan Gunn was appearing today, without his ponytail at . . . ."

In the best possible 'hair' today - gone tomorrow tradition, Bryan kept one step ahead of the media. When you least expected it, the ponytail would be there, whilst on other occasions it would be gone. When Bryan went to the U.E.A. in November for a cheque presentation on behalf of the Leukaemia Research Fund, the ponytail went with him. But, a few weeks later sitting next to Ian Botham on 'A Question Of Sport', it had disappeared again.

One of the ponytail's last official appearances was at Wycombe Wanderers for the third round of the F.A. Cup. Travelling home with a 2-0 victory under their belts, the team began to look for a Cup mascot, and Bryan's ponytail fitted the bill nicely. Following that match, the press began to write about the ponytail as Bryan's lucky charm. "It won't be cut until we're out of the Cup," was the battle cry. Unfortunately, being drawn against Manchester United in the next round meant that the ponytail's future would be short. Sure enough, having been beaten at Carrow Road, Bryan made the long trip to the barber's shop, where the now infamous 'hairloom' finally bit the dust.

If the ponytail had been a good luck charm, then the good luck certainly hit the floor along with Bryan's flowing locks. The next weekend saw City at home to Liverpool, a game during which Bryan was shown the red card for intentional handball outside his area. As he made his way towards the early bath, no doubt he glanced towards the opposite goal mouth where Bruce Grobbelaar stood, still sporting his own ponytail and ribbon.

Rumours abounded the following week. Had Bryan really trimmed his hair as a result of being knocked out of the Cup? Or was it Mark Robins' comments on television when he referred to Bryan's 'F.A. Cup ponytail?' Possibly it was Alex Ferguson's threat to telephone Bryan's mum and tell her of her son's new talking point. Or was it simply, knowing that he would be facing Bruce the following week, that Bryan had remembered that October day at his golf tournament. Maybe this town really wasn't big enough.

"O.K. Bruce, go for your comb!"

Susan Gunn, who has helped Bryan's appeal beat every target.

A Big Day For Little Matthew

It was a chance remark, made on the spur of the moment, that led to little five year-old Matthew Goddard's big day. Acting as a page boy at a wedding reception held at one of the function suites at Carrow Road, Matthew looked out onto the pitch and remarked, "I wish I could be a club mascot".

A neighbour, who overheard the remark, decided she would go straight into action. As soon as she got home she wrote to the football club, on behalf of Matthew, asking them to help his wish come true. Matthew's name went into the hat along with everybody else's and, sure enough, just two weeks later he was drawn out and invited to lead the Canaries out at their home game against Sheffield Wednesday in February this year.

For Matthew it was a dream come true. Just two years earlier he had been diagnosed as suffering from leukaemia, and had been receiving treatment at Addenbrookes along with Bryan's daughter, Francesca, on ward C2. In May 1993, he had undergone a bone marrow transplant, receiving the bone marrow from his seven year old sister Emily. Now, almost a year later, he was well on the way to recovery and eagerly looking forward to his moment of fame.

However, when the big day finally came, Matthew suffered a sudden attack of stage fright. His mum, Delia, remembers how Bryan helped to calm young Matthew's nerves.

"Matthew stopped running when he got onto the pitch and stood still. Bryan turned round and went back for him, taking him by the hand. Matthew's illness had slowed down his growing, a little, and he looked so small alongside Bryan as he led him to the penalty area".

After posing for a few photographs, Bryan invited Matthew

to take a few shots against him, allowing him to beat him with a delicate side foot.

"When Bryan let Matthew score, his little face lit up and he was beaming," said Delia. "I just sat in the stand with tears pouring down my face".

Since that day, Matthew and his family have become regulars at all of City's home games, although Matthew has eyes for only one player. "Whenever I look at Matthew," Delia said, "he's staring at Bryan, he never seems to look anywhere else, even when the ball's down the other end. Bryan has had such an impact on him, it's amazing".

Needless to say, Matthew now has just one ambition for when he grows up - he wants to be a goalkeeper like his hero. "Whenever he gets the chance, he wears his football kit," said Delia, "his eyes light up and he recreates the moment he scored past Bryan. I know it sounds daft, but since that day, Matthew seems to have taken huge steps forward in his recovery, he's far more enthusiastic about everything and it's almost as if Bryan's given him a new zest for life".

And it's not just whilst he's awake that Delia's noticed a difference, "After all his treatment, Matthew used to have dreadful nightmares and rarely enjoyed a good night's sleep," she explained. "I know people will say it's just a coincidence, and it probably is, but since the day he was a mascot, Matthew has never had another nightmare. It's as if he got rid of them all on the pitch that day".

It's easy, in this day and age, for people used to dealing with the public to merely go through the motions and treat one person very much the same as another. That accusation could never be levelled against Bryan. As Ian Botham said in his foreword, "If you're looking for heroes, you find them in people like Bryan Gunn". If you're not convinced, try asking little Matthew.

A day when dreams came true.

The Flying Scotsman

Most people who have studied the history of transport at school will have heard of the 'Flying Scotsman'. It's unlikely, though, that they would have expected to have seen their own version of this legendary engine, at Carrow Road, in February this year. However, as the digital clock above the 'Barclay' goal moved deep into injury time, delighted City supporters were treated to their own Canary edition of the famous train.

With only seconds to go, City were a goal down to Sheffield Wednesday and looked like ending their sequence of six consecutive league draws in the wrong manner. With almost the last attack of the match they had won a corner and were, perhaps, facing their final chance of salvaging a point.

As the ball floated high into the Wednesday goal mouth, the City strike force suddenly gained an unexpected addition to its ranks. Mimicking his long distance run when Gossy had sent Bayern Munich out of Europe, the charging figure of Bryan Gunn crashed into the Sheffield area. Out jumping everyone else, Bryan got the merest of touches to divert the ball across the box whilst, at the same time, completely flattening Rob Newman who, seeing only a red flash, must have been convinced that he'd just won a penalty.

As the ball bobbled around in the ensuing confusion, Bryan continued to bewilder the Sheffield defence until, suddenly, the ball fell at the feet of Chris Sutton who gleefully slotted home the equaliser.

Smiling broadly after the match, Bryan said, "I just wanted to create a bit of havoc," which was a bit like Sir Christopher

Above: Rob Newman gets that crashing feeling whilst,
Below: A keeper too many in the Wednesday box.

Wren saying he fancied a bit of D.I.Y. when he rebuilt St. Paul's Cathedral.

If it was havoc that Bryan was after, then this was one occasion when he certainly got his wish. It's difficult to know who was more surprised at his sudden appearance in the 'wrong' area. Certainly, the Wednesday players looked thoroughly confused when they discovered an extra keeper jumping around their six yard box, but the City team seemed more amused than shocked.

"I just laughed when I saw Bryan," said Chris Sutton. "I laughed even more when I scored," he added.

Certainly one group of people who didn't know whether to laugh or cry were the bookmakers who, up until now, had never considered including Bryan's name in their first goal scorers list. From now on the odds would have to be drastically reviewed.

The game ended all square at one each, but it was Bryan's last minute actions that remained the major talking point for some days to come. The green flash against Bayern Munich had now been joined by the red flash against Sheffield Wednesday. What colour the next flash would be was anybody's guess, and when and where it would appear remained an equally guarded secret.

Football or cricket - it's all the same to Bryan.

Guest Appearances

Whilst Bryan spent most of his spare time during the last year raising and collecting money for his own appeal, there were also occasions when he was invited to participate in other leukaemia and cancer activities. Seeing how money, already collected, was being used, and the good that it could do, must have given him great encouragement.

Like England cricketer Ian Botham before him, Bryan had helped to firmly bring the cause of leukaemia research to the forefront of people's minds. It came as no great surprise, therefore, when the Leukaemia Research Fund invited him to present a cheque, on their behalf, to the University of East Anglia.

Under the leadership of the Dean, Dr. Ian Gibson, the University was rapidly gaining a reputation as one of the major research centres into the causes and treatments of leukaemia and cancer. Accordingly, the L.R.F. was planning to provide the University with a grant of £88,238 to help fund new research.

When Bryan was first approached and asked to present the cheque he was delighted. Dr. Gibson was an ex-Scottish professional footballer and he and Bryan were already good friends. Indeed, at the football memorabilia auction, a few months earlier, Dr. Gibson had successfully bid for the signed Celtic club football which now held pride of place in his office.

And so, in November last year, Bryan and Susan were guests of honour at the cheque presentation. Although at this stage it hadn't been announced, Bryan had already decided to donate £60,000 from his own appeal fund to the U.E.A. to establish the new Francesca Gunn Laboratory. It was with double pleasure, therefore, that he handed over the L.R.F. cheque to Dr. Gibson. Whilst his appeal would allow a new laboratory to be built, this donation would fund vital research, some of it, no doubt, in the Francesca Gunn Laboratory, to be undertaken.

The research was hoping to find a kinder form of treatment for leukaemia and cancer sufferers. If successful, it could end the sickness and trauma often associated with chemotherapy and other forms of treatment. Dr. Gibson confirmed he was 'optimistic' about its potential whilst Dr. David Grant from the L.R.F. explained its benefits. Describing the project as being at the 'cutting edge' of research, he went on, "At present, treatment given to sufferers attacks all the cells in the body, causing such side-effects as nausea, hair loss and mouth ulcers. This new research will, hopefully, allow us to selectively attack" the leukaemia and cancer cells whilst ignoring the healthy ones".

Having devoted so much of his time to raising funds for research, Bryan must have been heartened to hear these optimistic thoughts.

A few months later, in March this year, Bryan and Susan were back at the University, this time as guests of the Cancer Research Campaign. The Duke of Gloucester, President of the Campaign, was visiting the University where, together with Bryan and Susan, he toured the school of biological sciences in the Cancer Research Unit.

Recognising Norwich as an International centre in the battle against cancer and leukaemia, the Duke praised local groups for the efforts they had made in their fundraising. Particularly impressed by the fact that Bryan's own appeal was funding a new laboratory at the University, the Duke commented, "Collectively, great progress is being made".

Much of that progress was being made possible by the response to Bryan's appeal and, whilst the occasion must have been emotional for them both, Bryan and Susan must have felt very proud of their achievements. When they had attended the L.R.F. presentation in November their appeal stood at £125,000. Now, just four months later, it was over £160,000. Nobody knew when Bryan and Susan would be back at the U.E.A. or how high their appeal would grow. One thing that was certain, though, was that there would be further visits and, just as certain, was that each visit would bring with it a new and higher figure.

Above: Bryan and Susan are presented to the Duke of Gloucester.

Below: Bryan and Susan with 'Big C' founder, Theresa Cossey.

Local disc-jockey Rob Chandler helps whip up some more funds for Bryan's appeal.

Fantasy Football

The one footballing craze that really swept the nation this year was 'Fantasy Football'. Suddenly, everybody could be a football manager with millions of pounds to spend. Every player was on the transfer list and available to your team and, as they all had fixed prices, you didn't need to be a master at the negotiating table to land your man. You simply stumped up the cash and the player was yours. After years of explaining down the pub, where your team's manager had gone wrong on a Saturday afternoon, you could now use that undoubted knowledge to create the finest side in the land. 'Fantasy' it may have been but, to the would-be managers taking part, it was deadly serious.

It all began as a weekly Radio 5 programme, which had rapidly developed a cult status. Spotting its obvious potential, the BBC soon transformed it into a Friday night show which became compulsive viewing for football know-alls up and down the country. Inviting twenty-two celebrity 'football managers' to take part, the BBC staged a mock 'auction' at which each 'manager' was given £20 million to spend and invited to bid for players as they came under the hammer. 'Managers' ranged from Lennox Lewis to Basil Brush and from Roy Hattersley to Peter Cook, and each was required to build a team without exceeding their £20 million. By the end of the auction some amazing sides had been put together.

It was the price paid at this auction which determined the value of a player in the many imitation leagues that sprouted up in the popular press. Bryan was bought at the bargain fee of £1.8 million by Mandy Smith, who obviously knew a bargain when she saw one, and that figure ensured that Bryan would be 'bought' by many would-be managers in the competitions that followed. It wasn't long before another Norwich hero announced that he had snapped up the services of Bryan. In the Daily Mirror competition, World Heavyweight Boxing Champion, Herbie Hide, named Bryan as his keeper explaining, "Apart from me, Bryan has got the best pair of hands in Norfolk".

However, it was the BBC show which attracted most attention with celebrity 'managers' appearing each week to talk about their teams. Unfortunately for Mandy, she soon found herself propping up the rest of the league, a position not helped by a sudden rush of goals against the City keeper.

Until now, Mandy had probably been best known as the child bride of Rolling Stone, Bill Wyman, and many viewers may have been forgiven for casting doubts on her ability as a football manager. Still, having recently traded Bill in for a younger version in the form of Millwall star Pat Van Den Hauwe, it might have been fair to assume that she was privy to some inside information.

However, Mandy's lack of success became more apparent as the season progressed and she struggled to explain away her problems when she appeared on the show. Like all good managers, she refused to single out any one member of her team for criticism, although she did once comment, "We're leaking too many goals at present".

Having been married to a Rolling Stone, Mandy should have been used to pressure but, as the gap between her and the rest of the league widened, she must have wondered if touring with the Stones was, in fact, less stressful after all.

"I keep telling him the only 'Satisfaction' I want is a clean sheet now and again."

Nice Goal – Shame About The Scorer

Most critics would agree, that English football is currently enjoying one of its finest periods for strikers. England team manager, Terry Venables, has confirmed this opinion by publicly stating that he has any number of permutations to choose from when assembling his teams.

Apart from City's own scoring sensation, Chris Sutton, the likes of Andy Cole, Alan Shearer and Ian Wright guarantee plenty of goals each week in the Premier League. Add to that list the non-English players like Eric Cantona and Mark Hughes of Manchester United, together with the ever-scoring Ian Rush of Liverpool, and you may begin to see why a goalkeeper's lot is not always a happy one.

After playing 41 league games, as well as 6 domestic and 6 UEFA cup matches, Bryan has had to face them all. Apart from those players already mentioned, the UEFA Cup games also brought Bryan face to face with such scoring legends as Dennis Bergkamp, Adolpho Valencia and Lothar Matthaus.

Week in and week out, Bryan has had to pit his wits against the very best that Europe could throw at him and, on most occasions he has come away with the honours. Many games have seen him come away with the plaudits and the headlines, as well as the 'Man of the Match' award and the customary bottle of champagne.

Indeed, towards the end of the season, one astonishing save he made late in the game at Manchester City was hailed by many critics as the best ever in the Premier League. Manchester City supremo, Francis Lee, who himself used to scare opposing keepers half to death, described it as equal to the famous save that Gordon Banks made from Pele in the 1970 World Cup finals.

Bryan modestly reflected on his season's work by remarking, "There were a few saves for me to make, but people will say that that's the keeper's job".

You would have thought, then, that Bryan's job description was already agreed by the team when they ran out onto the pitch. "Keeping out the opposition".

However, sometimes it wasn't just the opposition that Bryan had to contend with. Desperate to get on the scoresheet, one way or another, some of his team-mates decided to expand the job description to include 'keeping out your own players'.

Gary Megson started the trend just before Christmas at Ipswich. Drawing 1-1 with only minutes to go, City seemed to be heading to collect just one point from a game that they had totally dominated. When Ipswich won a last minute corner, Bryan would have been confident that, with the help of his defence, the ball would be safely cleared. No so! Jumping high above the Ipswich forward line Gary planted a delightful header well past the reach of Bryan into the top corner of the net, giving Ipswich a most unlikely winner.

Next it was the turn of Chris Sutton, who was surely scoring enough goals at the other end, not to need to plant one past his own keeper. However, when West Ham were awarded a free kick just outside the City penalty area at Upton Park, it was Chris who lined up on the end of the defensive wall. Allen of West Ham may well have claimed the goal, but it was most definitely the delicate flick of Chris which sent the ball skidding into the opposite side of the next to which it had been originally aimed, leaving Bryan scrambling desperately, and in vain, across his goal line.

Sweeper Ian Culverhouse was the third Canary to beat Bryan when, a fortnight later, he slipped one home on behalf of Liverpool. And, although it took another couple of months, Colin Woodthorpe joined the own-goal club when he pushed home the winner for Spurs. Finally, seven days later, Robert Ullathorne became the final member of the famous five when he finally beat Bryan at home to Southampton.

In a game that witnessed no less than nine goals, Robert really pushed Bryan's reflexes to the limit. His first attempt to catch out Gunny failed when his diversion came back off the post and was gathered up by a grateful Bryan, but he made no mistake with his second attempt when he rattled home the first of the Saint's five goals.

There must have been some discussion in the dressing room as to whether the players should be issued with compasses as part of their standard equipment. Failing that, the idea of painting arrows on the pitch to remind players which way they should be shooting was, no doubt, mooted. Whatever else was decided, Bryan was certain to have pointed out that he had enough problems with worrying about the likes of Matthew Le Tissier, without having to keep one eye on his own defence.

Happily, most own goals were cancelled out by successes at the other end of the pitch. Indeed, only a few weeks after getting the scoring bug for Liverpool, Ian Culverhouse scored his first ever league goal for City, in over 300 games, when he poked one home against Everton. Such was his surprise that Ian admitted afterwards that he had forgotten what to do to celebrate!

Robert Ullathorne made amends in the very next match at Manchester City, and even the harshest critic would probably agree that Chris Sutton was allowed just the one at the wrong end. As for Gary Megson and Colin Woodthorpe, - well there's always next season.

"So let's go through it once more".

Above: A light-hearted moment during the fundraising.

Below: WBO Heavyweight champion Herbie Hide collects the 'Presidents Trophy' after captaining Wroxham F.C. to a 6-3 victory over Poringland in a game that raised £450 for Bryan's appeal.

What Me Ref?

The idea of labelling Norwich a 'dirty' side would, to most football observers, appear somewhat fanciful. Better known for their attractive passing game rather than a 'stop 'em at all costs' attitude, City are one of the game's better ambassadors. As previous winners of the 'Fair Play' award it is unusual for them to be shown a card to match their famous yellow Canary shirts, and almost unheard of for them to see one the same colour as Bryan's favourite red jersey.

So it comes as something of a surprise, therefore, to look back on the season and discover that no less than three City players, including Bryan, were sent off. Add to that another City star admitting he was lucky to stay on the pitch, and you begin to get the feeling that, somewhere along the line, things didn't go quite as planned.

It all started in the local derby match against Ipswich at Portman Road last December. Having only been on the pitch for a matter of a few minutes as a substitute, Lee Power found himself late with his challenge on Phil Whelan. The referee had little doubt which pocket to reach for and, in the 87th minute, City received their first red card of the season. An own goal three minutes later by Gary Megson added to City's misery and suggested that the last three minutes of a City game could prove to be eventful.

Certainly, Bryan got to know that last three minute feeling when, a few weeks later in February, he received his own marching orders in the 89th minute for deliberate handball at home to Liverpool. Having been beaten to the ball by Steve McManaman, who then chipped it over Bryan's head, an instinctive hand shot up to push the ball away. Goalkeeper or not, even Bryan couldn't get away with handball a good ten yards outside his own area.

Just a fortnight later and one minute earlier, in the 88th minute at Swindon, Jeremy Goss must have felt that he was staring his own red card in the face. Believing that John Moncur was about to take a swing at John Polston, Gossy promptly engaged Moncur in their own version of a 'Bash Street Kids' bundle. Two minutes later when the match came to an end, a relieved Jeremy remarked of the referee, "I don't know how he came to not send me off".

Whatever it was that John Deehan had decided to put into the pre-match refreshments, last February, it was certainly working. With one off and one lucky to stay on in the space of two weeks, it was only another four days before City said goodbye to their third red card player, making it a month to forget.

The final member of the unwanted 'Red Army' was John Polston who also made his early exit in the last minute. This time, however, it was the last minute of the first half during the home match against Blackburn when City were reduced to ten men. Leaving his team-mates a man short for the entire second half against the team battling to overtake Manchester United at the top of the league, could be considered a little unthoughtful. However, the Canaries responded magnificently and even took the lead in the second half before having to finally settle for a 2-2 draw.

Having already had three players suspended for their final European match against Inter Milan, City's disciplinary record was not living up to its usual high standards.

Bryan's own sending off was particularly disappointing as the subsequent one match ban prevented him from being the only City player to appear in every league, domestic cup and European game last season. However, his biggest problem may still be to come, explaining how, as a goalkeeper, he came to be sent off for handball!

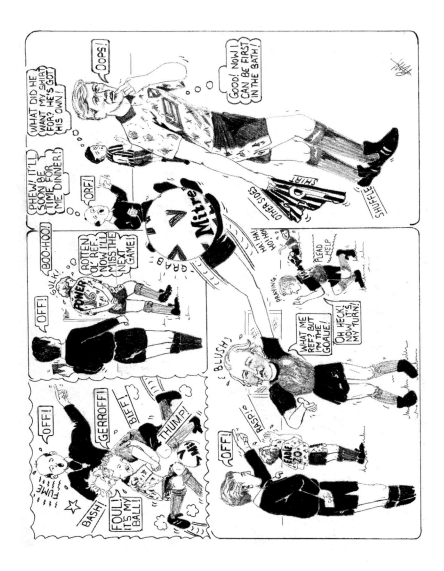

End Results

Dr. Ian Gibson, an ex-Scottish professional footballer, is now Dean of the biology department at the University of East Anglia. His department has been chosen to receive massive funding from Bryan's appeal. Here he talks about his hopes of what can be achieved as a result of that funding.

What kind of work will you be undertaking in the Francesca Gunn laboratory?
We'll be doing what I think is very hotshot research in terms of finding new cures for leukaemia. Research which, I believe, will also help in the treatment of cancers. We have a novel approach to these problems, based on an understanding of the molecular biology of cancer cells. This approach has now been recognised by grants from the Leukaemia Research Fund as well as monies from local charities such as Bryan's appeal.

How important are people like Bryan Gunn to your research?
They're absolutely essential. Without Bryan's support we couldn't do anything like this at all. We wouldn't be able to compete nationally or internationally with any of the other big hospital groups. If we had a medical school in Norwich, of course, it would be different, but as it is Bryan's support has taken us from division four to division one in terms of

being able to get on with the job. His funding will allow us to purchase new advanced equipment with which to carry out our research and also to increase our number of researchers. Since Bryan announced that he was giving the money to us we've gone from three people working in the lab to twelve. We've had people coming to join us from the Ukraine, we've got somebody who's joined us from Moscow and, in the summer, we've got somebody coming from Turkey to work with us. That's how attractive we've been able to make ourselves. Without the Gunn money we would never have been near to that.

With the new equipment that you're now able to purchase along with the extra researchers, how close do you believe you are to finding a cure for leukaemia?
Well, of course, there are many different types of leukaemia, but as for the particular childhood form that we are involved with, I should think we will have prospective cures within four or five years. And, you know, a lot of this optimism has been brought about by the support of Bryan and Susan. I just feel fantastic warmth towards Bryan, not just because he's Scottish or anything like that, but it's a recognition that he lives in a city like Norwich, he plays for the local football team and I work for the local University. We both have that old Scottish football culture behind us and to be able to combine it in this way is quite unique. Everybody at the University is extremely grateful, especially the people who work in this department. There's a pride because we're doing this. If you ask the people who work in this department what they're most proud of, I think you'll find that many of them, especially those who come from Norfolk, will say that it's the association with the Bryan Gunn Appeal. It makes them feel that they're working in a very special place. And that can't be bad, to build moral like this. So it's not just the work that we're doing which is so special, it's also the way it's making people feel who work in the department. There's a great sense of pride here because of the Bryan Gunn Appeal.

Final Thoughts
(An Interview with Bryan Gunn)

"Bryan, if we can start by talking about your appeal. I know that prior to launching your own appeal you were involved in raising money for various leukaemia charities, what was it that made you decide to start your own appeal?"

"Well, we were having dinner one night with Keith Colman and we decided to have a little go at raising some money for leukaemia research. It started off with the 'Gunn's Golden Goals' and we weren't sure how much money we would raise so we set an initial target of £10,000 and crossed our fingers. The first game we played was at Tottenham where we lost 5-1 so it didn't get off to too good a start, but then we beat Leeds 4-2 and that really got the ball rolling. We finished off the season quite strongly and through the pledges we raised about £12,500. But there were so many other events being organised we decided to keep the appeal open and it got turned into the Bryan Gunn Leukaemia Appeal".

"When you decided to get away from just the 'Gunn's Golden Goals' you organised some pretty major events, I'm thinking about the football memorabilia auction, the golf day and the gala performance of 'An Evening With Gary Lineker'. How difficult were these to put together?"

"Well, they were difficult but at the same time they were enjoyable. With the first one, the football auction, we sat down and wrote to most of the clubs in the Premier League and the Football League as well. A lot of the memorabilia came from outside the Premier League. After that it was just a case of getting everything co-ordinated and Keith and Gill at the office put in a lot of work there. Then with my contacts in the football world, I was busy on the phone to people like Bruce Grobbelaar and Brian McClair to get stuff sent down from Liverpool and United and, you know, they all came through.

The auction night, itself, was a tremendous success. We raised over £10,000 and there were a lot of people there. Unfortunately it clashed with the Lord Mayor's Procession where myself and the City team were taking part in the parade and, you know, that was a bit of a shame because it meant a lot of people were out on the streets that night who might have come to the auction, but it was still a great success.

The golf day was easy to arrange, with me being a golfer. Sprowston Park were great and donated the course for the day and, again, it was mainly a case of phone calls. With my contacts with players who enjoy a game of golf, it was just a case of getting everyone down there for the day. It was unfortunate that we had a couple of last-minute call-offs through Bruce Grobbelaar and Chris Woods, but to be fair to everyone else, they all went out of their way to turn up and that made it a success.

The 'Evening With Gary Lineker' performance was mainly out of our hands as we've not really got any contacts with the theatre world. Peter Wilson and all the people at the Theatre Royal were tremendous and, again, everything was given free of charge. All the actors and actresses came for nothing and we managed to put on a gala performance that will never be repeated. We changed things so that on the night we had two or more people acting out the same plot which wasn't in the original script. But it all seemed to work very well on the night. Lots of people turned up and it was another great success".

"All three events were obviously very successful, did you enjoy any one of them more than another?"

"I don't know, that's difficult to say. I mean, I was very involved with all three. The auction night was very enjoyable, we had Stuart White and Rob Chandler there as auctioneers.

Launching the appeal.

The golf day went very smoothly, we had that in October and it was a tremendously sunny day. It would be difficult to put your finger on one of them and say which was the most enjoyable. Even down to the theatre night, that was quite a night as well".

"I was going to ask you about that night. When you appeared on stage how did that compare, in terms of nervousness, to say playing in front of 100,000 or so people?"
"Well most of the lads turned up quite late in the afternoon. We were actually due to start at 7.30 but most of the lads got there about 4 o'clock to rehearse their little bits. That wasn't too bad and everyone was pretty calm at that stage. But when the crowds started to arrive, and you know we had almost a full house that night, then one or two of the lads began to get a bit nervous. I had to come on at the end and I wasn't sure if I'd get my bit right, so that was quite nerve racking too. I think I'd probably prefer to stick to playing in front of the 100,000's in places like Mexico or wherever, rather than in front of the 2,000 that were there that night".

"You had an impressive line-up of stars to help you get through that nervousness".
"That's right, we had a lot of people who are regulars on television. There was Samantha Beckinsale, who's now on television quite a lot, we had Billy from the Boswells (Bread) and there was James from the Medics. Since that night they've all been on national television and for us to have appeared with them in some way is quite good. It's something that the lads always mention at the training ground after they've seen them on T.V. the night before".

"I understand you intend to repeat the golf day next year, is that going to become a regular event?"
"Yes, I hope so. You know, after the last golf day a lot of people were telling us how much they had enjoyed it and that if there was another one to put them down for it. So we're in the process of arranging another at Barnham Broom in

September 1994 and we'll be making sure that it's as good as, if not better than, the last one. We'll be trying to get a lot of different sporting personalities and celebrities for the next one which will hopefully draw in the crowds better".

"Obviously all the events already planned will bring in a lot of extra money. I know most of the money already raised has gone to funding the Francesca Gunn laboratory at the U.E.A. Do you have any firm plans as to where the future money will go?"

"Well, the laboratory will obviously need refunding in the future. It's not just a case of ploughing in, say, £60,000 to set up, it will need further funds to buy new equipment and so on. We've also spent some money at Quidenham hospice and a lot of money has gone to the Norfolk & Norwich hospital to help Dr. Barbara Jennings in her research. She's also researching future cures and looking at ways of speeding up the results of the blood counts so that the doctors can have these quicker when children go into hospital. But we're also open to any other areas which need funding and we'd like to hear from them all to see if there's any way in which we can help to fund them".

"Do you think the fund will carry on indefinitely?"

"It probably will now. It's something that we never thought of originally when we set a £10,000 target. But now after a year there's over £170,000 in the fund. Obviously a lot of that will come out during the summer to fund the U.E.A. laboratory and that's something we would like to be able to refund. So yes, I hope we'll be able to keep it going."

"If we can turn to your other career, that of a goalkeeper, have you found that your work as a fundraiser has changed your approach to the game in any way?"

"No, I don't think so. I think my approach to the game has always been the same. Obviously my work with the fund has kept me busier than before. I spend a lot of time accepting cheques after training and before matches, but that's not a problem. I mean it's been impossible for me to get out to all the events which have been arranged so we invite people to bring their cheques down to the ground, and at least that way they get a souvenir photo as a keepsake. I would love to go and pick up all the cheques but with the football career and training that's just not possible".

"Staying with football, for a moment, despite the disappointing second half of the season, the European games in the first half ensured it was one of the most exciting seasons ever at Carrow Road. What were the high-points for you?"
"I think it has to be the European games. Our first game against Vitesse Arnhem was a high-point as it was our first game in Europe. We put on a good performance and won 3-0 so that was a good night. The best nights, though, were probably the Bayern Munich games. You know, we went to the Olympic Stadium where they hadn't been defeated in European football for years and went on to beat them. And to show just how good that victory was they've just gone on to win the German league. And the night back here when we got the 1-1 draw at Carrow Road was just fantastic. It's the best night I can ever remember in the eight years I've been here. The crowd were amazing, they really got behind us even when we let in the early goal. The reaction from the fans got the reaction from the players, and that's a night I'll never forget".

"I know you've got a particularly good rapport with the Carrow Road crowd. How much does it lift you when they get behind you?"
"It helps enormously, and it's something we find when we go away to the big grounds. When the crowd get behind their players it really inspires them. You know, whether they're shouting for you or against you it can really lift you during a match. We may take 3,000 or so supporters to any away game and when they start singing and shouting it can really help you. If we got that at Carrow Road every week I'm certain it would inspire the players on to better things".

"We've talked about the high-points of the season, what were the low-points for you?"

"Obviously the disappointing end to the season was something that the players didn't want. We'd have liked to have been higher up the league or challenging for one of the cups. Getting knocked out of the F.A. Cup by Manchester United so early was a disappointment. We had the home advantage but couldn't make it pay. I think getting knocked out of the UEFA Cup and getting beaten by United were probably the low-points".

"With United going on to win the F.A. Cup and Inter Milan winning the UEFA Cup, does that soften the blow a little?"

"Well, you could say that. It means we obviously played against two quality teams. As I said we beat Bayern Munich and they've gone on to win the German league so it does show that we can compete against the better teams. We just need to do it more consistently and also to do it against teams from the other end of the league".

"Leaving the pitch for a moment, how much did the Mike Walker affair affect the team?"

"I think the fact that, at the time, we were having such a good season here, together with Mike's popularity with the press and the fact that Everton are such a big club, that the headlines were greater than they might otherwise have been. The way things happened doesn't sound too nice with hearings and appeals and the like, but none of that had anything to do with the players. Obviously, we were upset to lose Mike as he's been a part of the greatest success that the club has ever had. We were also disappointed that we couldn't carry on that success for John Deehan, as John's been part of that success too. Mike Walker brought him in as his assistant two years ago and it's a pity that we couldn't finish the season off in the way we'd started it".

"One thing I've always wondered is what do you keep in the bag that you take to your goal at the start of each match?"

"It's a bag that I get from my sponsors. I keep a spare set of gloves in there, my hat and I've also got a picture of Francesca, Susan and Melissa that I kiss before I go out. I've also got a silver locket in there with some of Francesca's hair in it. A lot of people think that when I go to my bag I'm eating something but I'm actually kissing my silver locket. This is probably the first time I've ever mentioned it. People always think it's chewing gum or something and ask, "What do you eat?" but it's a little silver locket that Susan got and it's got some of Francesca's hair in it and I keep in in the bag all the time. I always make sure when I finish a game that it's still in there, you know, in case it's fallen out".

"When you were younger did you always want to be a goalkeeper?"

"I think my mum's the best person to answer that question. She'll tell you I used to go through so many pairs of trousers. You know, I'd be diving about at school, even on the cement and the tarmac, so I was always going home with holes in my trousers. Then my mum devised this plan where I could go to school with a pair of shorts on under my trousers, then at playtime I'd take off my trousers and be able to dive about in the mud and grass. Then I'd go back into school with dirty legs but it wouldn't matter because I'd put my trousers back on over the top. So yeah, I was always going to be a goalkeeper when I was younger. I fancied myself as an outfield player as well, but I was so tall and liked getting dirty so it was always going to be a goalkeeper".

"How did you get started professionally?"

"My father was in charge of the primary school team, he used to take the primary 6's and primary 7's and they were the ones who were normally in the school team. I used to go along as a primary 4 or 5 and join in with the training. I always used to get a game at the end of training and always managed to get in goal. Then one week the first choice

A year of two managers

Above: With John Deehan at the celebrity golf day

Below: No hard feelings after beating Mike Walker's Everton 3-0 at Carrow Road.

goalkeeper couldn't make it and I got to play in goal. Then I got signed by Aberdeen, I was playing in an amateur match for a men's team and they came to watch me. We got beat 6-0 that day but I must have made some good saves because they invited me down for a trial. That went well and I signed for them as a 14 year old".

"When you first started did you model yourself on anyone? Who would you say was the greatest keeper you've ever seen?"
"That's pretty difficult. When I first started playing Ray Clemence was the top goalkeeper at Liverpool. When I came down to England I was fortunate to play against Ray as well as people like Bruce Grobbelaar, Neville Southall and Peter Shilton and that's something I'll always be proud of. This year I've played against some of the Italian greats in the games against Inter Milan, Genoa and Italy. That's something I'll never forget and I've got a nice set of three jerseys which I'm going to put in a frame. That's something I'll be able to take away when I've finished playing".

"Talking about finishing, goalkeepers have a reputation for staying at the top longer than the average outfield player. You'll be 31 this year, how much longer do you feel you can stay at the top?"
"Well, that's obviously down to myself in the way I look after myself and maintain my fitness. Nowadays you find players in the Premier League playing on until they're 37 or so; Peter Shilton went on until he was 40. Obviously these players have looked after themselves over the years and it's up to me to do the same. I've got another two and a half years left on my contract, so obviously the club believe I can go on that long and I'll be hopeful of continuing after that. I hope to continue to play in the first team, that's the only place to play football but it's mainly down to myself."

"When your playing career finally does come to an end, do you have any firm plans about what comes next?"
"I'm looking at various different things at the moment. I'm

looking at getting into college and doing some course work to get my brain working again. I left school at 16 with some good marks and O levels but I didn't really continue anything after that. These days young players are advised to carry on with some college work but in those days we just got straight into our football. I've got a few spare afternoons now and I'll be looking into courses on computing or marketing or something like that".

"Does football management interest you?"
"Yes, I think so. These days you often find that top players slot straight into management. Obviously, I want to carry on playing as long as possible but there may well come a time when I'd like to try my hand at management".

"You could possibly copy Peter Shilton and try your luck as a player-manager?"
"That's right, but it's a difficult one when you start letting goals in and you've got to decide to drop yourself".

"You've been on television and radio a lot during the last 12 months and seem to have a natural talent in that area. Does that type of career interest you at all?"
"Yes, it does. A lot of people have said that I do that kind of thing well and if an opportunity arose in that area then I'd have to look at it. I enjoy being on television and the radio, it's not something I feel nervous about. You know, a lot of people get very nervous and don't think that they can speak but I enjoy doing it".

"You're certainly not nervous on television. I remember your appearance on 'A Question Of Sport' when you over-ruled Ian Botham. Thankfully you were right."
"Yes, that's right. Ian was the captain and it was probably one of the few times he's been over-ruled. It was a motor racing driver on the picture board and Ian thought it was Michael Schumacher. I'd been reading a motor racing book that morning and was certain it was Jean Alesi and went for him

instead. Luckily, I was right, even Johnny Herbert was struggling to get it and he was the Formula One driver on the other side".

"You obviously have a very busy schedule between your work as a goalkeeper and your fundraising activities. On the odd occasion that you do get a night off, how do you like to spend it?"
"Myself and Susan like to go out for a meal with friends, although this season that's been quite difficult with the number of midweek matches we've had. So it's been mainly round to people's houses for a nice meal and a bottle of wine. It's a good way of unwinding from what's been a really high profile season with lots of memorable games. It's a way of getting yourself prepared for the next one".

"Is the television on much at home?"
"Every now and then Susan will give me some real stick because I sit down and watch all the soaps. You know I start with Neighbours and go through Eastenders and Coronation Street and so on. Then there's all the sports programmes that I watch so yes, there is quite a few hours spent in front of the T.V."

"So you're a closet soap fan?"
"Yes, definitely".

"Do you get the chance to go out to the cinema or theatre much?"
"Quite often. If we can get the chance we like to get out to the top movies that are on at the time. Susan's very keen on the theatre but we've not had much of a chance to get there in the last year, but it's something we will do again in the future".

"Does music play a major part in your life?"
"Yeah, I've got a monster collection of CDs. I'm quite lucky to have a CD player in both cars so we get the chance to listen to them not only in the house but also while we're driving

"When the crowd get going it can really lift you".
Bryan at Liverpool for the last game ever in front of The Kop.

along. Also if we have people around for dinner we always put music on".

"Is there a particular area of music you prefer?"
"I like a lot of soul. Luther Vandross is a big hero of mine, I've got a lot of his albums. We've also got a lot of classical ones as well which we find quite stimulating. If we're sitting around reading we'll put them on in the background".

"How about humour, any real favourites?"
"I like Harry Enfield, I enjoy watching his sketches, I think he's very funny. I used to enjoy Billy Connolly but he's a bit off the scene now. Rab C. Nesbitt, he's another Scot who's had a lot of funny sketches on T.V."

"Two people you've mentioned there are fellow Scots, is there a particular type of Scottish humour?"
"Yes, I think it's just the black humour that appeals to us".

"Returning to your fundraising for a moment. Assuming the appeal continues to be supported, will there come a time when you have to restrict your own involvement? I'm thinking of the way Ian Botham targets, say, four major events a year and leaves the rest to the back up team".
"Yes, I think that's probably right. What we managed to do in our first years was to have 3 or 4 major events backed up by lots of cheque acceptances. We weren't able to get out and see as many people as we would have wanted to but, learning by last year's experience, that's probably the way it will have to continue. If people continue to support us in the way they already have I just don't see how I could possibly attend all, or even some, of the events that take place. We need to establish some sort of happy medium whereby people are still getting thanked and receiving recognition for their efforts. You know, I'd love to attend more events but I think Ian has realised over the years that you just can't be everywhere. So we'll try and keep the major events and invite people to make their presentations at those."

"Talking of Ian not being everywhere, one place where he will be later this year is walking through Wales on his latest walk for Leukaemia Research. I've heard whispers of you joining him".

"Yes, I'd love to. Again it's down to the football commitments. The walk starts, I understand, at Goodison Park so the best thing for me would be if we were to play Everton away that weekend. That would be unbelievable. Or failing that away to Liverpool would be almost as good. But failing that I'd still love to join him either at the start or even half way through. It's something that I tried to do on his last walk but with Francesca's illness I couldn't make it. I was disappointed at that but I'm really hoping to be there this year".

"I know Ian would be proud to have you with him. Bryan, thanks very much".

"You're welcome".

Gunn Shots 1993/94

GAMES PLAYED:
  53 – 41 Premier League
  6 UEFA Cup
  4 Coca Cola Cup
  2 F.A. Cup

TIME ON PITCH/GOALS CONCEDED:
  Time on pitch 4,769 minutes (allowing for last minute missed after being sent off against Liverpool).
  Goals conceded : 70 average of 1 every 68 minutes.

HALF HOUR SPREADS:
  11 conceded in 1st half hour
  32 conceded in 2nd half hour
  27 conceded in 3rd half hour

1st/2nd HALF SPREADS:
  25 conceded in 1st half
  45 conceded in 2nd half

EARLIEST/LATEST GOALS:
  Earliest: 4th minute by Valencia of Bayern Munich at Carrow Road.
  Latest: 90th minute own goal by Gary Megson at Ipswich. 90th minute by Monkou of Southampton at Carrow Road.

PENALTIES:
  3 faced - beaten by all.

CLEAN SHEETS:

14 plus 3 other occasions when held out until final 10 minutes.

BEST PERIODS:

347 minutes between 54th minute at Ewood Park, Blackburn and 51st minute at Hillsborough, Sheffield.

429 minutes between 13th minute at Goodison Park, Everton and 82nd minute at Stamford Bridge, Chelsea.

Both periods included 3 clean sheets.

WORST 10 MINUTES:

51st minute - 60th minute 13 goals conceded.

71st minute - 80th minute 13 goals conceded.

WORST MINUTE:

37th, 42nd, 58th and 70th. 3 goals conceded in each.

QUICKEST CONSECUTIVE GOALS:

58th minute and 61st minute at Hillsborough against Sheffield Wednesday.

55th minute and 58th minute at Carrow Road against Aston Villa.

GOALS CONCEDED PER GAME:

0 goals - 14 games

1 goal   - 18 games

2 goals - 14 games

3 goals - 5 games

4 goals - 1 game

5 goals - 1 game

NIGHTMARE DEPARTMENT:

3 conceded against Sheffield Wednesday in 10 minutes.

4 conceded against Queens Park Rangers in 35 minutes.

5 conceded against Southampton in 46 minutes.

"Watch out Bryan, 37th minute again".

Norwich City Results 1993/1994

Date	Opponents	Home/Away	Score	Minute Goals Conceded
15.8.93	Manchester United	Home	0-2	25th, 57th
18.8.93	Blackburn Rovers	Away	3-2	7th, 54th
21.8.93	Leeds United	Away	4-0	
25.8.93	Ipswich Town	Home	1-0	
28.8.93	Swindon Town	Home	0-0	
1.9.93	Sheffield Wednesday	Away	3-3	51st, 58th, 61st
11.9.93	Wimbledon	Home	0-1	56th
15.9.93	Vitesse Arnhem (UEFA Cup)	Home	3-0	
18.9.93	Q.P.R.	Away	2-2	33rd, 83rd
22.9.93	Bradford City (Coca Cola Cup)	Away	1-2	24th, 46th
25.9.93	Everton	Away	5-1	13th
29.9.93	Vitesse Arnhem (UEFA Cup)	Away	0-0	
2.10.93	Coventry City	Home	1-0	
6.10.93	Bradford City (Coca Cola Cup)	Home	3-0	
16.10.93	Chelsea	Away	2-1	82nd
19.10.93	Bayern Munich (UEFA Cup)	Away	2-1	40th
23.10.93	West Ham United	Home	0-0	
26.10.93	Arsenal (Coca Cola Cup)	Away	1-1	79th
30.10.93	Arsenal	Away	0-0	
3.11.93	Bayern Munich (UEFA Cup)	Home	1-1	4th
6.11.93	Sheffield United	Away	2-1	42nd
10.11.93	Arsenal (Coca Cola Cup)	Home	0-3	14th, 34th, 65th

20.11.93	Manchester City	Home	1-1	59th
24.11.93	Inter Milan (UEFA Cup)	Home	0-1	80th
27.11.93	Oldham	Away	1-2	47th, 62nd
4.12.93	Manchester United	Away	2-2	30th, 42nd
8.12.93	Inter Milan (UEFA Cup)	Away	0-1	88th
13.12.93	Leeds United	Home	2-1	67th
18.12.93	Ipswich Town	Away	1-2	7th, 90th
27.12.93	Tottenham Hotspur	Away	3-1	73rd
29.12.93	Aston Villa	Home	1-2	55th, 58th
8.1.94	Wycombe Wanderers (F.A. Cup)	Away	2-0	
15.1.94	Chelsea	Home	1-1	42nd
24.1.94	West Ham United	Away	3-3	37th, 45th, 83rd
30.1.94	Manchester United (F.A. Cup)	Home	0-2	18th, 73rd.
5.2.94	Liverpool	Home	2-2	52nd, 76th
13.2.94	Arsenal	Home	1-1	33rd
19.2.94	*Swindon Town	Away	3-3	16th, 45th, 50th
23.2.94	Blackburn Rovers	Home	2-2	31st, 58th
26.2.94	Sheffield Wednesday	Home	1-1	75th
5.3.94	Wimbledon	Away	1-3	37th, 64th, 74th
12.3.94	Q.P.R.	Home	3-4	49th, 64th, 70th, 84th
21.3.94	Everton	Home	3-0	
26.3.94	Coventry	Away	1-2	28th, 70th
29.3.94	Newcastle	Away	0-3	37th, 50th, 70th
2.4.94	Tottenham Hotspur	Home	1-2	55th, 76th
4.4.94	Aston Villa	Away	0-0	
9.4.94	Southampton	Home	4-5	44th, 57th, 63rd, 72nd 90th
16.4.94	Manchester City	Away	1-1	45th
23.4.94	Sheffield United	Home	0-1	31st
30.4.94	Liverpool	Away	1-0	
7.5.94	Oldham	Home	1-1	13th

* Bryan did not play in this match as he was suspended.

The Final Goal.